WRITE A
BOOK FOR ME

The Story of Marguerite Henry

World Writers

WRITE A BOOK FOR ME

The Story of Marguerite Henry

David R. Collins

MORGAN REYNOLDS Incorporated

Greensboro

WRITE A BOOK FOR ME
The Story of Marguerite Henry

Photos courtesy of the
Marguerite Henry Estate

Library of Congress Cataloging-in-Publication Data
Collins, David R.
    Write a book for me : the story of Marguerite Henry / David R. Collins
       p. cm. - - (World Writers)
    Includes bibliographical references and index.
    Summary: Describes the childhood, writing career, and personal life of
the author Marguerite Henry, known for her books about horses.
    ISBN 1-883846-39-0
    1. Henry, Marguerite, 1902- -- Juvenile literature. 2. Women authors,
American--20th century--Biography--Juvenile literature. 3. Children's
stories--Authorship--Juvenile literature. 4. Horses in literature--Juvenile
literature. [1. Henry, Marguerite, 1902-. 2. Authors, American.
3. Women--Biography.] I. Title. II. Series.
PS3515.E5784Z54   1999
813'.54--dc21
[B]   99-11667
                                                        CIP

This book is dedicated to Miss Louise Deckers,
who reined in a fifth grader who liked to horse
around by introducing him to the grand and glorious
world of words of Marguerite Henry.

Contents

Marguerite Henry

Chapter One

Last But Not Least

Somewhere and sometime in history, there probably lived a child who enjoyed receiving "hand-me-downs." For the benefit of readers in "only child" families or for readers in families having lots of money for new clothes, "hand-me-downs" are articles of clothing worn by one child until it is outgrown, then passed on to a younger sibling. Sweaters and shirts, and dresses and skirts have been known to last for decades in some families, moving from one child's closet to another.

Yes, there has undoubtedly been one child in place and in time who enjoyed receiving "hand-me-downs." But it was definitely NOT Marguerite Breithaupt, the final child born to Louis Breithaupt a respected publisher, and his wife Anna, an equally respected housewife, on April 13, 1902 in Milwaukee, Wisconsin. Having three older sisters, Marguerite was the recipient of countless hand-me-down items, short on style and long on repair. If it was good enough for Marie, Elsie and Gertrude Breithaupt to wear, it was good enough for little Marguerite. At least Anna Breithaupt thought so. As for the girls' only brother, Fred, he simply looked on with an impish delight when one item of clothing was handed down to the next sister. "Oh, do I have to wear this?" was the usual moaned exclamation of the sister inheriting the garment, and Anna Breithaupt would be ready with a patient and soothing, "But it looks so good on you."

By the time she was seven, Marguerite Breithaupt had a closet full of hand-me-downs. Most she had accepted with little complaint, knowing it was family tradition. But Marguerite was convinced she did NOT look good, no matter what her mother said, in the astrakhan coat that Gertrude, or Trudy, had outgrown. No doubt when the item was purchased for the eldest daughter, Marie, during the previous century, the coat was impressive. Yet the icy rains and heavy snowstorms of Wisconsin winters are not easy on the fleecy lambskin of astrakhan coats. Neither are children hurling snowballs, or the coat's occupant sliding down hillsides without sleds, or sprawling on the ground to make snow angels. By the time young Marguerite inherited the garment from Gertrude, the astrakhan coat was torn and tattered, a lonely survivor of countless freezing seasons. Marguerite hated the coat. She was "as skinny as an eel," according to the boys at school, and the coat hung heavy on her small frame. In magazines and newspapers, she studied the pictures of

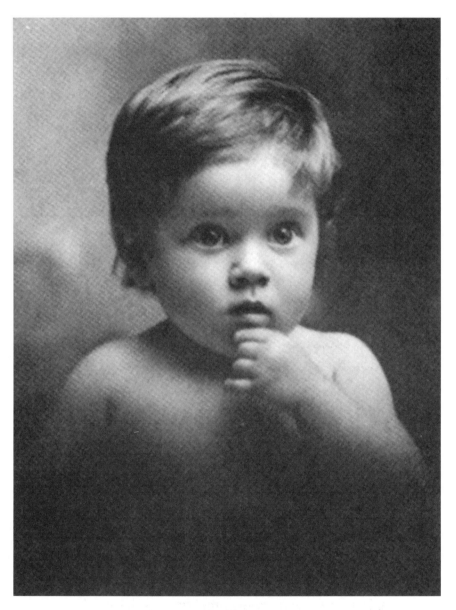

Marguerite was born on April 13, 1902.

Alice and Ethel Roosevelt, the two daughters of President Theodore Roosevelt. How elegant the two girls looked in furtrimmed collars and bright red cloth coats. Never did those two girls wear anything like the astrakhan coat that draped around the scarecrow shoulders of Marguerite Breithaupt.

Each winter morning before school Marguerite voiced some complaint about the coat at the breakfast table. It was "so old"—it was "so ugly"—and "No one else has to wear a coat like that." Family members ignored the moaning and groaning, leaving the girl totally frustrated. Being the youngest of the five children present, she also felt the least noticed.

One day, James Sherman, the newly-elected United States vice-president, visited Milwaukee and rode in a motorcade. Schools had dismissed for the special occasion. Later, Marguerite found a way to grab special attention among the family by announcing at lunchtime that the famed Mr. Sherman had leaned over and "shooken hands" with her.

Eyes widened and jaws dropped open. The vice-president of the United States shaking or "shooking" hands with little Marguerite? Unbelievable! Astonishing! Surely the girl should never wash that hand again—or she should have it cast in bronze like the five sets of Breithaupt baby shoes displayed on the living room coffee table.

No one was more impressed than Marguerite's

mother. "Oh my dear child," Anna Breithaupt sighed, shaking her head in radiant wonder. "You see, it wasn't your coat he noticed. It was your inner beauty that shone through."

Heads nodded in agreement. Sisters and brother thought quickly of whom they could tell, how their friends would be so impressed with their little sister. It was so exciting, almost impossible to believe!

Impossible was just what it was. Vice-President-elect Sherman had indeed ridden in a motorcade down the streets of Milwaukee. Yes, he had leaned over to shake hands with a young girl standing along the way. But it was not Marguerite Breithaupt. It was her schoolmate rival, Dilla Blumquist, who was honored with the vice-presidential handshake.

"I lied!" Marguerite wanted to stand up and shout. "It's just that no one ever notices me and I have to wear that awful coat and Dilla Blumquist gets everything."

There was so much Marguerite wanted to say, but the words did not come. Looking at the sparkle in her mother's tired eyes silenced the young girl. But one thing was certain after that day. No longer would she complain about having to wear the astrakhan coat. To Marguerite, it was small enough penance to pay for telling such an untrue and foolish story.

Being the youngest, Marguerite was expected to take orders from everyone in the modest but cozy structure the Breithaupt family called home. She learned quickly that if her mother might not give in to a request, one of her "motherly" older sisters might. Neighborhood friends knew this as well. When they hollered for Marguerite to come out and jump rope or play hopscotch, the girl immediately asked her mother. Sometimes the answer was no.

"Ask one of your other mamas," someone would holler back. Marie, Elsie and Trudy were easier to persuade, especially when Marguerite promised to exchange her dessert for permission. Her older brother Freddy was always willing to let her go, too. It was not easy being the lone brother with four sisters. Getting even one of them out of the house, however briefly, made life easier.

Whenever Marguerite complained about being the last and littlest of the Breithaupt children, someone told her the story of the duckling. The day Marguerite was born followed a heavy April rainstorm. The usually quiet waters of a nearby creek became wild and overflowing, snatching countless duck eggs along the shoreline. Only one egg remained when the storm ended. The shell exploded, releasing a strong and cheerful young duckling. It took a front position before a collection of ducks and drakes and led the entire brood as it marched along its way.

Again and again young Marguerite listened to the story. How well she knew the story's clear moral. The duckling was lucky to have so many elders around, ready to give swimming, diving and fishing lessons. She was lucky too, to be surrounded by so many elders ready to assist her in whatever she tried to do.

But then again, the duckling never had to wear hand-me-down clothes or ask permission to go out and play. But she did.

There were many other stories told around the Breithaupt supper table each evening. As a publisher, Louis Breithaupt rubbed elbows with a variety of people and kept pace with the current events of the day. Each evening he shared news with his family, and young Marguerite listened to every word from the father she adored.

Mr. Breithaupt talked about a man named Henry Ford, whose automobile factories were producing thousands of Model T Fords. This single car design led production and sales of all automobiles. Ford loved to say that his "customers could have any color of the Model T as long as it was black." A smiling Anna Breithaupt announced she'd heard women drivers could soothe their "automobile wrinkles" by applying slices of raw cucumber on their faces. Marie, Elsie and Gertrude released a mixed chorus of groans, but Marguerite giggled with glee.

One night, each of the Breithaupts found a surprise waiting on their dinner plates. It was a copper coin, just like those they spent on peppermint sticks at Nickleson's Confectionary around the corner. But this coin had a new face on it, that of Abraham Lincoln. They all wondered what had happened to the Indian head penny?

"Is it real money?" a skeptical Marguerite asked, holding her coin an inch from her eye. "Can I buy candy with it?"

Her father smiled and nodded. "It might be spent for something more worthwhile," the man answered. "But spend it you may."

A new Lincoln head penny was a special gift. But the best present young Marguerite received arrived on Christmas Eve in 1909. She tossed and turned all night long and was the first one out of bed the next morning. Still in her ankle-length nightie, she raced into the kitchen. She could not speak as she gazed on the magnificent sight in the corner.

There sat a little red table and chair. In a cream pitcher on the table were pencils, three red, two green, and one yellow. The erasers on the end were untouched by human hand—or mouth, for that matter. Marguerite ran to them and pulled them from the pitcher. Yes, the pencils boasted points as sharp as Mama's sewing needles. So often she had to move her lined paper off the kitchen table so Mama could start supper, or so one of her sisters could do her homework. Now Marguerite had her own table with its own chair, and pencils, too.

The thrilled girl moved forward, her eyes widening. There, tied to the table with knitted string, was a gleaming pair of shears. No, they were not baby scissors, but rather grownup cutters that could slice through even thick paper. And there was an enormous jar of paste, too, with a brush handle which seemed to say, "Use me! Use me!" At the end of another knitted string was a paper punch, just perfect for pressing holes in paper.

Marguerite glanced at her father, her face unable to hide her joy. And then she looked to her mother, as she took in the next treasure on the table. There sat her mother's pin tray that used to sit on top of her dresser holding her favorite pansy brooch. Now, a minature mound of paper clips filled the container. To top it all off was a brand new pencil sharpener on the corner of the table.

Marguerite's hands reached down to several tablets of colored paper piled in an even stack. Every color of the rainbow was there, waiting to be covered with words and stories. As she lifted the top sheet, she read her father's no-frills script:

> Dear Last of the Mohicans,
> Not a penny for your thoughts,
> but a tablet.
> Merry Christmas!
> Papa Louis XXXX

Marguerite smiled, rereading the note. *Last of the Mohicans* was the name of the great novel by James Fenimore Cooper, a book Papa had read aloud to her on Sunday afternoons. It told of the final days of an American Indian tribe. But Papa had meant the inscription for her, the last of the Breithaupt family. On this day Marguerite did not mind being the youngest and the 'last." It made her feel important.

Carefully, the proud and thrilled young girl folded Papa's note and opened the top drawer of her new Christmas table. She slipped it under a horseshoe paperweight. Never did she want Papa's beautiful handwriting to be mixed up with her own scrawlings.

Whirling around, Marguerite made a loud and clear declaration so that all present could hear. "I will join the writer's trade!" the seven-year-old girl proclaimed.

No doubt somewhere in the world Mark Twain shivered with fear, hearing on the wind of his new competition. Beatrix Potter probably trembled too, as well as Jack London, and all the rest whose stories had won them world attention as authors. On this Christmas was born a new weaver of words, a Miss Marguerite Breithaupt of Milwaukee, Wisconsin.

Picking up one of the grand pencils, the girl sniffed the wood as if it were fine perfume. She happily snipped the shears in the air, proud that the blades were not blunt-ended like a child's. She snapped up a piece of pink paper from a tablet. Snip! One quick slice and one sheet became two pieces. Whipping out the paste brush, she swabbed the two halves together.

Marguerite's delight was contagious, each member of her family caught the girl's smile and laughter. The girl fought to hold back her tears. Everything was right! At last she had her own world—not a hand me down or a have to share world—but a world of her own—a writing world. She ran to her father and hugged him. There was no place safer than his arms. She wanted to hold onto this moment forever, but she knew it would pass.

And yet, as she gazed back at the writing table and all of its treasures, a thought slipped onto the pages of her mind. Perhaps, just perhaps, she could write about this moment. Then it would never be gone. It could be saved in words.

Chapter Two

"We are pleased to inform you. . ."

The corner in the kitchen where Marguerite spent every available minute was never officially labeled "Marguerite's Corner," but it might as well have been. Hour after hour she labored there. A nasty bout with rheumatic fever kept her home from school for a time, but whenever she felt strong enough, she began writing. It was good therapy because minutes slipped quickly into hours.

Marguerite loved to write accompanied by the sounds of work in the house. A hired girl helped her mother clean and cook, and the two made the kitchen come alive with clinking and clanking of dishes and pans. In the distance Marguerite could hear Marie at her sewing, the machine letting out a special song as the older girl seamed and stitched. Elsie and Trudy took turns playing the piano, while outside, Freddy tossed a baseball on the roof, then let it drop into a glove. Papa liked a quiet house when he came home from work, and Marguerite delighted in the fact that her writing made not a sound.

Marguerite's hand flew over the page. She wrote of her family, of her father's countless memorized Shakespeare speeches and her mother's way of arranging flowers into grand table centerpieces. She wrote of Marie's fingers, stitching and embroidering lovely dresses on the sewing machine, then using those same skillful hands to make Bach, Beethoven and Brahms come alive on the piano keyboard. She wrote of Elsie's way of pulling a loose tooth by tying it to a string on a doorknob and slamming it. She wrote about Freddy grabbing her hand and running so fast she felt she was flying. And whatever she wrote, there was Trudy, always ready with just the right word, its proper meaning and spelling. Freddy visited her writing area often, shaking his head. It amazed him that someone could want to put words onto paper voluntarily. Writing to him was work, a task assigned by teachers determined to torture those who sat on hard wooden desks in their classrooms.

"You—you like sitting here like this?" he would ask. His question was cloaked in disbelief. "You are doing this because you want to?"

"Yes, Freddy, I do." The girl shook her head. "You like playing catch off the roof? You do that because you want to?"

Marguerite thought it was not a good comparison. But she could think of nothing else to say. She returned to her tablet, deliberately scribbling on the top line of the paper BROTHERS ARE PESTS in big letters. Such actions usually sent the intruder on his way. It worked this time!

Despite Freddy's occasional teasing, Marguerite knew she was lucky to have such a wonderful family. She was convinced that no youngster had a jollier time of growing up.

On Saturdays, Marguerite visited her father at his publishing house. The sound of the printing presses was music, and she scampered between rows of paper stacked high. Louis Breithaupt regularly brought home manuscripts, galley proofs and sections of books in process. Marguerite loved to write at her own special spot in the kitchen while her father worked nearby. Sometimes she helped him read too. Anna Breithaupt's favorite reading pleasure was a monthly magazine called *The Delineator*. The periodical featured current news, recipes, tips for successful family living and wholesome stories. When her mother told Marguerite the editor wanted children to submit stories about any of the four seasons for possible publication, Marguerite brightened. She loved a challenge. Which season to write about—spring, summer, autumn or winter? Several times the girl started writing. Several times the wastebasket received her efforts. Finally, a birthday party offered her the inspiration she needed.

When Marguerite was a teenager, she loved to visit her father's publishing business.

It was October, and Wisconsin was bathed in a rich and colorful Indian summer. A classmate, Beth, was having a birthday party. Marguerite journeyed into the country with friends, leaving the noises and mood of the city far behind. The girl's home sat in a wilderness of trees, and on this special day the wind whirled the golden and scarlet leaves into corners around the house and barn. A game of hide-and-seek sent the birthday guests racing in every direction, their feet crunching into the brittle leaves. Spotting a big mound of maple foliage, Marguerite slid beneath and covered herself. Seconds passed, and then became minutes. She did not move, sure that she would never be found.

Suddenly there was a sniffing sound in the leaves. It was a dog, Beth's dog, Omar. Given one of Marguerite's party gloves to pick up the scent, the canine proved a shrewd detective. The laughter that followed was cheerful and loud, but a call from the house brought the guests running. Marshmallows melted on-top of the hot chocolate, and candles burned like sparklers on the birthday cake. The frosting was so thick Marguerite wished she'd had a long tongue like Omar's to lap it up.

What a grand day it was, full of colors and sounds and smells—all the senses that made writing come alive. The words came quickly, and Marguerite recaptured all the details of the birthday party on paper. Calling her manuscript simply "Hide-and-Seek in

Autumn Leaves," the girl carefully addressed an enve-
lope to the editor of *The Delineator*. She mailed the
entry and then put it out of her mind.

Weeks passed. Finally, at the end of two months,
Marguerite received an answer from the magazine editor. "We are happy to inform you. . . ." the letter began.
Marguerite could not believe her eyes as she read further. They wanted her story—the people at *The
Delineator* wanted her story about the birthday party!
Enclosed was a check for twelve whole dollars. The
editor suggested Marguerite use the money for summer
camp. Again Marguerite read the letter, looking back
and forth to the check. The girl felt dizzy. Writing was
fun—and it was such a pleasant way of making a living. Writing grabbed and held the girl. At eleven, she
renewed her promise to be a writer, a published writer.

Marguerite took the editor's advice. In the summer
of 1913, she journeyed to Illinois's Lake Pistakee to
spend a week with other girls between the ages of eight
to twelve. Her slender, tall frame put her eye-to-eye
with the oldest girls attending.

But it was not the other campers that captured
Marguerite's interest. It was Miss Laura Bertelson, the
camp leader and Marguerite's Sunday school teacher.
Beautiful beyond words, poised, and sensitive, Miss
Bertelson had the secret of making even the shyest girl
feel relaxed.

As the girls gathered around a glowing campfire on their first night, the camp leader was ready with a way of pulling the group together. "Let's all tell our hobbies," she said. In the brightness of the flames, her face revealed eyes wide in expectation. Not to share, judging by the woman's voice, would break her heart.

One by one, the girls revealed their hobbies. "I ski!" came one answer. "I swim, forty laps!" came another. "I like fancy skating." "Tennis is the best!" There were nods of agreement, light laughter after some admissions. Only "cooking" brought a unified "boo", perhaps because some of those assembled were too often asked to help with that chore.

Finally, it was Marguerite's turn. She swallowed deeply, very conscious of a throat that felt dry and empty. No one here would understand. No one. They didn't have a father who owned a publishing house and made books. They wouldn't understand the thrill of seeing a blank sheet of paper go through a printing press and come out covered with stories and dreams, with information and ideas. Marguerite glanced around to the expectant faces.

"My hobby," she stuttered, "is words."

There. It was out. Everyone else had a hobby of action. Skiing, swimming, skating—even cooking. They were all "do something" hobbies. As she soaked up the silence around her, the awesome sounds of nothing, she wanted to throw herself onto the campfire and burn to ashes.

But then it happened. A warm cheerful voice broke through the thick quiet air. "What a coincidence!" Laura Bertelson exclaimed, her head nodding agreement. "I like to play with words, too. What kind do you like, Marguerite?"

Once again, her throat tightened. It was too late to win the respect of her fellow campers, of that Marguerite was sure. "Tin-tin-nabulation," she squeaked out.

"Oh!" the camp leader responded, not thrown for a moment with the odd, gigantic word. "You're thinking of Poe's tintinnabulation of the bells, bells, bells."

At once the butterflies flew from Marguerite's stomach. It was not that Laura Bertelson merely knew what she meant. The camp leader answered with such enthusiasm, like she and Marguerite shared some special bond. Joy instantly replaced the shame that had filled the young girl. For Marguerite, no one was more of a true heroine than Laura Bertelson.

But despite her admiration for Miss Bertelson, Marguerite suffered from homesickness all week. She missed her family. Determined not to let her feelings show, she threw herself into the camp activities. She swung a ping-pong paddle with vengeance, and dog-paddled through the lake with record speed. No one noticed the tears she shed—she hid the longing to be home well.

Marguerite thrilled at the sight of her little red table and chair when she came home. During her absence, her father had whittled stilts for the furniture to keep up with their occupant's ever growing frame. Marguerite felt tall, just like a budding author should, and she gazed at her kitchen corner with new fondness. It looked so businesslike, so warm and inviting. Only one thing was missing—a bulletin board with wise sayings on it. Her father had one down at his office. It was covered with clever thoughts spoken by wise people, such as ". . . that's a valiant flea that dares eat his breakfast on the lip of a lion." The great playwright, William Shakespeare said that about courage, and there were many others posted.

Marguerite had her own collection of wise sayings, but she knew better than to tack them into her mother's newly-painted kitchen walls. That action would be very unwise. So the quick-thinking girl used half her allowance for a week, purchased colored pushpins, and pressed the paper sayings to the margin of her table with her thumb.

Next to mother's milk books are the best nourishment.
—*Lawrence Clark Powell.*
The more you read the better you write.
—Anonymous
Words can build great castles or create empty dungeons.
—*Ralph Waldo Emerson*

Each statement was worthy of more than a moment's reflection. Satisfied with each one, Marguerite always sought new additions. Her search took her roller-skating to Milwaukee's North Side Branch Library every other day. The building was a mile away from the new family home at 801 Cramer, a short mile indeed, for a girl whose love for books grew with each visit. From worn pages sprang Heidi of the Alps, Daniel Boone of the wilderness, and Peter of the land of windmills. With her imagination she became each of them as she read, yodeling in the mountains, hunting in the woods, and sticking a finger in the dike to save her country.

On one crisp afternoon, Marguerite pretended she was Hans Brinker on skates, who was the hero of the book she clutched. Locked in her own thoughts she did not see the speeding motorcycle heading toward her. The passing cyclist threw out his arm to knock her out of the way. Sent sprawling, she luckily suffered a minor head cut that was quickly bandaged. The book she'd been carrying was not so easily mended. Marguerite dreaded facing the librarian, a Miss Delia G. Ovitz. Each book from the library was carefully marked with a warning: "Books must not be defaced. Any injuries beyond ordinary wear shall be made good to the satisfaction of the librarian. The holder of any card having losses charged against him is debarred the privileges of the library. Failure to comply with this rule will forfeit all privileges of the library."

No library privileges? Just the thought of it brought tears to Marguerite's eyes. She had to have a new book every other day. It was like eating and sleeping. No library privileges? It was like finding a "no vacancy" sign on the gates of heaven!

A trembling Marguerite Breithaupt presented the battered copy of *Hans Brinker* to Miss Ovitz. The librarian, like a mother tending her child with a scuffed knee, examined the book closely. Then the woman took Marguerite by the hand and led her to a small room behind the stacks of books. Atop a crowded table were labels, pastes, tapes and shears. There were pens and inks, shellacs and a vise. It was a hospital for books, a repair shop for damaged spines and torn pages.

With loving devotion, Miss Ovitz became a doctor, leading Marguerite through the step-by-step process of mending the injured volume. Once the operation was complete, the librarian looked at the book with a mother's relieved concern.

And Marguerite Breithaupt knew she had a new heroine in her life: Miss Delia G. Ovitz. Truly, this woman was Queen of the Realm of Books.

Chapter Three

A Fellow Named Sidney

"I come here to find myself, it is so easy to get lost in the world."

Marguerite stared up at the sampler hanging above the checkout desk. How many times had she read those words? Fifty? Maybe one hundred. Beneath the words was the name John Burroughs. Whoever this man is, Marguerite thought, he feels the same way that I do. The needlework was clearly Miss Ovitz's handiwork, much like the swirling initials on her white blouses or the miniature colorful bouquets on her sweaters.

Every other day after school Marguerite visited the library. Her father once told her about some famous person who had read every book in his local library while a child, and Marguerite vowed to be the second. Biographies and mysteries were her early favorites, but when she discovered the western adventures of Zane Grey, she could not get enough. Someday she vowed to own a ranch where stallions and mares could romp and play and have countless fillies and colts. At times,

Marguerite felt stuck inside the city, just as she was stuck inside that dreadful astrakhan coat. She welcomed any chance to visit the country just to glimpse the horses nuzzling the grassy soil for a morning snack or prancing across the field toward a farmhouse. Whether it be a graceful pony in the spring of its life or a weary wagon-pulling stock animal entering its final winter, Marguerite saw beauty in the creature.

Yet to own a farm someday, with horses in a stable, required money. Marguerite waged a campaign at home to let her get a job while going to school. She promised to keep her grades up and to do her assigned family chores. Louis and Anna Breithaupt opposed the idea at first, but when a job opened up mending books at the library, their resistance tumbled. For two hours after school each day and five hours on Saturday, Marguerite became a book doctor. Under Miss Ovitz's careful eye, the girl stitched and sewed, pasted and erased. She was even allowed to collate books the library put together for patrons. Of course, every page had to be counted to make sure it was in order.

Marguerite started off fine. She breezed through the two hour stints after school. Saturdays posed more of a challenge. Knowing she would be there longer caused Marguerite to take her time. "1-3-5-7..." The counting became boring quickly. Reading a book's pages was so much more fun than counting them. One volume soon pulled Marguerite in, demanding her full attention. A

Marguerite at age sixteen, when she worked as a "book doctor" at the public library.

dark shadow suddenly appeared on the page she was reading. Marguerite gazed up. Miss Delia Ovitz's usual soft brown eyes blazed.

"You, Marguerite, will have to find other work," the librarian decreed in a voice curt and brittle. "You may put on your coat and leave."

Devastated, the girl slid from her stool. But her finger kept her place in the book she held. She looked up at Miss Ovitz.

"I'll go," Marguerite answered humbly. "But oh, Miss Ovitz, you've got to read this! Your sampler man, John Burroughs, wrote it."

The librarian looked puzzled. "My sampler man?"

Extending the book, Marguerite pointed to the essay "Summit of the Years." Then the girl turned and trudged away with legs which had never felt so weak. Slowly, she slipped into the astrakhan coat and buttoned down the cocker spaniel earflaps on her cap. Sitting on a chair, she put on her overshoes, pressing each of the eight buckles firmly down. She grabbed a cloth from the table, soaking up the tears that streamed down her face. The cloth smelled of library paste, that wonderful sticky substance that she would never smell again.

The sound of heels clicked behind her, and without warning, Marguerite felt hands clasping her shoulders. In a soft and gentle voice, Miss Ovitz quoted the John Burroughs words Marguerite had so recently discovered herself. "I go to books as bees go to the flowers for a nectar that I can make into my own honey."

Marguerite smiled, once again enjoying the thought. The librarian turned her around.

"Child, child," the woman said, her voice as soft as rose petals. "I shall stitch another sampler for the library. And you shall help me hang it when it is done. Now, off with your coat and get to work. Mind that you count this time, not read."

While Marguerite's wish to become a writer never wavered, she flirted with acting in high school. She added her drama teacher, Mrs. Anholt, to her ever-growing collection of role models. As they read plays in the classroom, Mrs. Anholt brought characters to life with dialogue that sounded so real. Words, words, and more words—Marguerite heard so many voices sharing their hopes and dreams, their anger and frustrations.

Miss Shaeffer, Marguerite's English composition teacher, helped put those words on paper in an organized way. Spelling and mechanics were the tools of the writer just as much as a camera and darkroom were the tools for a photographer. When one student protested that a popular writer of the time, F. Scott Fitzgerald, knew little formal English and was a bad speller, Miss Shaeffer's reply was brief.

"When you write as well as F. Scott Fitzgerald," the English instructor declared, "I shall overlook a spelling error here and there. Until then, keep your dictionary and grammar text close at hand."

Marguerite accepted Miss Shaeffer's comments as law, and the girl obeyed every one. The high school newspaper, *Mercury,* seldom appeared without a story she had written.

Following her graduation from high school in 1920, Marguerite knew she wanted to keep writing. But it was not a practical goal as a profession, according to her father, who had seen many writers struggle to make a living. Teaching English seemed just the right choice. She enjoyed children, loved literature, and could write as a pastime. If she proved successful at getting her work published, then she could think more seriously about the area of professional writing. Having no desire to leave home, Marguerite enrolled at Milwaukee State Teachers College and the University of Wisconsin in Milwaukee.

During the summers, Marguerite escaped with her older sisters to a fishing camp in northern Wisconsin. Louis Breithaupt could seldom escape from work for any length of time, but Marie and Elsie both married fishermen who were glad to enjoy the waters of Hubert's Resort. Trudy came too, and when she became engaged, brought her fiance. It was there Marguerite met Sidney Crocker Henry.

Sidney Henry was a business sales manager, and Marguerite discovered he loved numbers as she loved words. Tall and slender, the bespectacled young businessman was clearly well-read, with opinions based on fact gathering. He attracted Marguerite's attention upon their first meeting. They spent the afternoons fishing and sharing their thoughts and even their future dreams. At night, they danced on the resort patio in the moonlight to the playing of a pianist whose piano needed tuning. Yet no sour chords could hinder a romance that grew with each passing day.

As the vacation time ended, Sidney invited the Breithaupts to his family's home in Sheboygan. Marguerite had never seen such a huge vegetable garden as the one the Henrys kept next to their rambling house. It was late summer harvest season, and over a lunch accented by homegrown corn on the cob and juicy, prize tomatoes, the conversation never lagged. But then it was time for farewells. Marguerite and Sidney parted, promising to meet at the resort in a year, same time and same place.

Sidney broke his promise. In less than a month, he came knocking at the Breithaupt front door in Milwaukee. Once inside, he impressed Louis and Anna Breithaupt as quickly as he had impressed their daughter. Marguerite was thrilled. Her father was ill, yet Sidney Crocker Henry brought fresh laughter into the house. Louis Breithaupt did not recover from his illness, but before he died, Marguerite wrote, "My father passed the torch to Sidney, who kept the flame of love for me burning all through our lifetime." Marguerite and Sidney were married May 5, 1923.

Sidney's job required travel—and lots of it. Up to this point in her life, Marguerite had seldom strayed from the confines of Milwaukee. Now she suddenly started playing travel hopscotch, joining Sidney as he went from one big city to another. She helped him write sales bulletins for his company too, her high school newspaper experience coming in handy. Although there was not much time to get settled in at any one location, Marguerite decided to try writing magazine articles. Sidney was more than supportive. When they arrived in Philadelphia, Marguerite looked over the list of local publishers and read them aloud to her husband. Maybe, she suggested, she should go visit an editor or two.

"Why not call on *The Saturday Evening Post?*" Sidney suggested.

Marguerite could not believe her ears. *The Saturday Evening Post* was one of the top magazines in the country! It was clear that Sidney Crocker Henry knew a lot about business, but he sure didn't know about writing.

Or did he? Once Marguerite got over her initial surprise, she decided to take her husband's advice. Armed with little more than courage, she visited the magazine offices and spoke with an editor. When she walked out, she had an assignment for a three part series, no less.

Marguerite and Sidney Henry were married on May 5, 1923.

Entitled "Turning Points in the Lives of Famous Men," she was to interview important figures of the times and share their ideas.

The assignment proved a major challenge. As she talked to different subjects, the one who impressed her most was the noted lawyer Clarence Darrow. At times it was unclear who was interviewing whom when they met together. As an attorney, Darrow was used to asking the questions. He shot them at Marguerite like a machine gun. She felt more like she was a witness in a courtroom rather than a woman seated at a table scribbling notes onto a tablet.

"Why are you more important than that mouse skittering across the floor?" Darrow demanded. Other questions were just as direct and sharp. The interview was a rugged interrogation for Marguerite, whose questions were far less pointed. Yet from her notes she put together an article that won praise from her editor—and readers too.

Marguerite and Sidney did not want to simply jump from place to place all the time. They found an apartment in Chicago. Travel arrangements were easy to make from the home base in America's heartland, and Marguerite was surrounded by plenty of libraries and research facilities. Her byline began showing up not only in the *Post*, but in *Reader's Digest*, *Forum* and *Nation's Business*. Editors found her easy to work with and willing to accept any assignment. She loved to

Marguerite enjoyed working outside at her cottage in Freeport, Illinois.

visit manufacturing plants, then share her observations in crisp, simple articles.

The move from the Chicago apartment into a white cottage in Freeport, Illinois, proved to be a major writing turning point for Marguerite. The Henrys hired a Finnish cook named Beda and her husband Effendi, who mowed the lawns and did handyman work. Much time was spent in the Henry kitchen where Beda braided ropes of dough and created delicious baked goods. Effendi whittled constantly, tiny flowers, wreaths and animals emerging from wood blocks of varying sizes. Marguerite listened as her two friends shared tales of their native Finland, and a book grew in her mind. She recorded the tales in a volume called *Auno and Tauno*, dedicated it to Beda and Effandi, and asked a neighbor artist, Gladys Rourke Blackwood, to try her hand at illustrating the manuscript. The manuscript and drawings found a receptive editor at Albert Whitman Publishing, and Marguerite Henry's first book appeared in 1940.

Children responded to *Auno and Tauno*. They asked their parents and grandparents to buy it at bookstores. They asked their teachers to read it aloud in school. Marguerite was delighted with the response. She had hoped young people would like her work. Now that they did, she knew they would be her special audience.

Marguerite and Sidney liked living in a small town, away from the fast pace of the city. But now that she knew she wanted to write books for children, Marguerite thought it might be better to live closer to Chicago. Albert Whitman Publishing was in Morton Grove, Illinois; Wilcox and Follett were Chicago publishers doing some fine works for boys and girls, as was Rand McNally Publishers. All were in or near Chicago.

On a driving expedition, Marguerite and Sidney came upon a little weathered ranch house. The village of Wayne, Illinois was only half an hour's drive west from Chicago. Yet it sat removed from the hectic pace of big city life. The couple agreed that they could drive into Chicago anytime they wished, and yet they could enjoy life in the country as well. Both Marguerite and Sidney had been raised in cities, but they had always loved the outdoors; the fresh air of the country, the birds and the animals roaming free. Together they headed east to Wayne, little knowing the surprises soon to come into their lives.

Chapter Four

Along Came Misty

As soon as Marguerite was settled into their new home in Wayne, she returned to her typewriter. Sidney insisted Marguerite have her own writing space and she created a small study, her own special retreat. Her slender fingers flew across the keyboard and manuscripts went sailing in the mail to editors across the country. Now, most of her writing was directed toward children. Few of her submissions came back with rejection slips, those dreaded notes of "We are sorry to inform you..." writers hate to receive.

Marguerite's earlier years served her well. Again and again she thanked her sister Trudy for making her search for just the right word in her writing. The days working at the Milwaukee Public Library proved valuable too. She knew how to research, whether it be information about a faraway country or a bird common to northern Illinois. She gathered facts like a peapicker picks peas, then slipped them into a lively presentation. With her words and the illustrations of a man named

Kurt Wiese, she took her readers from Argentina to the Virgin Islands, from Brazil to New Zealand in a series called *Pictured Geographics* published by Albert Whitman Publishing. Each children's book made her feel she was reaching young readers and making new friends.

Just as Sidney traveled for his work, Marguerite did the same. She liked visiting other parts of the country and meeting new people. "Every person is a character," she told friends, "and each of their lives is a story. I listen as a person when someone is talking, but I also listen as a writer. You never know when a new lively tale might come along."

Such a "new lively tale" came along when Marguerite met eighty-nine-year-old David Dean Hewitt, a crusty old storyteller from the Vermont hills. Hewitt told a tale about a schoolteacher named Justin Morgan, and Marguerite soaked up the story like a thirsty mare at a fresh water stream. It seemed Morgan traveled from Vermont to Massachusetts to collect a debt from a farmer. Having no money, the farmer paid Morgan with two horses, a fine colt named Ebenezer and a runt pony named Bub.

Marguerite focused on Bub for her writing. She created a central character from one of Mr. Morgan's students, Joel. The boy takes a liking to Bub and trains him to be a champion puller. When Bub is sold, the new owner mistreats him. Joel works hard to rescue

Bub, and the boy's efforts pay off. At the end of the story, Bub carries President James Monroe on his back. Bub's descendants became know as Morgan horses in honor of the schoolteacher who had treated the horse so kindly.

Marguerite's words galloped onto the paper with little hesitation. Her research brought the time period, the late 18th century, to life. She captured the mood and the majesty of the rural Vermont hills, and Joel, Bub, Justin Morgan and all the rest reached into the reader's mind and heart. While looking around for a possible illustrator, Marguerite came upon a slender picture book called *Flip* by Wesley Dennis. It was a gem, each illustration a delight, and it was Mr. Dennis's first offering. She wondered if he might do the pictures for her own full length effort, *Justin Morgan Had a Horse*. It was worth a try, she thought, so she sent him a copy of the manuscript. They set up a meeting in the Barbizon Plaza Hotel in New York City. When they spotted each other in the reading-writing room, Dennis zipped across the floor, the manuscript under his arm.

"You Marguerite Henry?" the man asked.

Somewhat overwhelmed, Marguerite nodded.

"I'm dying to do the book," Dennis said, "and I don't care whether I get paid or not."

So began a collaboration that would last for seventeen books. The team of Henry and Dennis would gain

Grandpa Beebe was a treasure house of information about the ponies on Chincoteague Island.

fans across the country and far beyond. Their creative minds worked together whether they sat at the same table or shared thoughts on the phone a thousand miles apart. Marguerite's words sparked Wesley Dennis's imagination, and his illustrations left her breathless at how he could perfectly capture her words.

Justin Morgan Had a Horse not only won the attention of youngsters, the book found praise waiting from professional critics as well. "Henry and Dennis are two peas in a pod," wrote one reviewer. "Fortunately, they are creative geniuses not peas, and the pod is a book, not a casing for a vegetable." Much to Marguerite's surprise and delight, *Justin Morgan Had a Horse* was named a Newbery Honor Book, a runner-up for the top juvenile writing prize in the nation.

Dr. Mary Alice Jones, an editor at Rand McNally in Chicago, was a regular guest to the Henry home in Wayne. Despite efforts to avoid writing as a topic of conversation in order to give the visiting Dr. Jones a brief respite, it always arose. Sidney listened for awhile, then gradually drifted off to a different part of the house, leaving the two word wizards to talk about their favorite subject.

On one such evening, in the spring of 1946, Dr. Jones made an unusual suggestion. She proposed Marguerite take a trip to Virginia that summer. There might be a story in the wild-ponies that lived there, and how they swam across the channel from Assateague

Grandma Beebe welcomed Marguerite to Chincoteague.

Island to Chincoteague Island. There might indeed, agreed Marguerite. But what would Sidney have to say about such a trip?

"Go!" were her husband's orders. But he had a suggestion too. "Take Blondie Coffie, the village equestrian, with you. With her experience she can help select the wildling I'm sure you'll bring home."

As usual, Sidney's idea was a good one. With local horse lover Blondie Coffie in tow, Marguerite set out for the east coast. She called up Wesley Dennis who lived in Warrenton, Virginia, and invited him along too. He happily accepted.

What Marguerite found was a fascinating event, Pony-Penning Day, which lent itself to exciting storytelling. Over 25,000 tourists watched as volunteers on horseback drove the wild ponies from Assateague Island across the waters to Chincoteague Island. An auction of the healthy foals allowed horse breeders and lovers a chance to purchase animals for a lifetime of love and care.

Marguerite, with Wesley Dennis at her side, immersed herself with the people on Chincoteague Island during her visit. She made close friends with the Beebe family, noting that every one of the household, from grandparents to grandchildren, made good writing "fodder." Grandpa Beebe was especially interesting, although the people of Chincoteague knew him as "Grandpa Wiry." He was a treasure chest of knowledge, a rich collection of tales and legends. As a writer trying to separate fact and fiction, Marguerite asked the old man how the wild ponies had originated on Assateague Island. Some believed an old Spanish galleon had shipwrecked off the island, sending the cargo of horses swimming for their lives.

Jumping down from his own stallion, Grandpa Beebe shook his head and stomped his foot. "Marg'ret!" he declared, his tone defiant and disgusted. "Facts are fine, fer as they go, but they're like waterbugs skitterin' atop the water. Legends now, they go deep down and pull up the heart of a story."

Grandpa Beebe spoke with such a crispness and good sense. He showed a natural instinct for what made a good story. Marguerite felt such a kinship with the old man. What a grand character he would make in a book. He was almost as wonderful as the tiny filly she had fallen in love with at first sight. The golden pony was so proud and perfect—and patriotic too! Why the animal had a white mark on her withers— right behind her neck—that looked just like a map of the United States. Marguerite named the fine creature Misty, knowing the filly would breed a million and one stories.

But when Marguerite asked to bring a new pony back to Illinois with her, Grandpa shook his head once again. This time, however, his voice showed compassion, and a kind sensitivity. "I ain't a-goin' to let you do it," he said. "A nursing young'un needs its mama. But when three-four months is up, I'll send her to you so's you can write yer story. Then when you're done you can send Misty back to Paul and Maureen, my grandkids."

Marguerite accepted the deal. She shook hands with Grandpa Beebe, noticing the man's grip was as strong as a pump handle. She was just as sure that his word was good too.

Once back in Wayne, Marguerite prepared for the "company" that was coming. She laid out plans for a three-horse stable. Although Misty was the only guest expected, it seemed foolish to build a structure for one horse. Anyway, the other stalls could house tack, hay, straw, a saddle and other equipment.

Marguerite busied herself with other writing assignments, yet she could hardly wait for the day when Misty would arrive. When the horse finally came, Marguerite could not believe her eyes.

It was a grim grey November day, drizzle and cold chilling the bones. The horse had made the journey by train, packed into a homemade wooden crate. Marguerite moved closer, slipping her hand between the slats. What was this? She felt wool, like a sheep. No, surely Grandpa had not sent the wrong animal. But where was the sleek silk coat Misty wore?

That first surprise was followed by another. When the expressmen delivered the Henry guest to the new

Marguerite based characters in *Misty of Chincoteague* on Maureen and
Paul Beebe.

stable and Sidney ripped open the front of the crate, Marguerite expected the pony to pop out happily. It was quite the opposite. Misty was so stiff-legged she could barely stand at all. Gently, Sidney lifted the filly out.

Marguerite stood in shock. Where was the beautiful filly from Chincoteague? This creature had no golden coat, no golden eyelashes, no United States map in white on her withers. This pony was nothing but a disfigured gray snowball.

Suddenly Sidney burst out laughing. "So this is the beautiful filly with a coat of gold! Humph! She looks more like a Siberian goat!"

Still convinced Grandpa Beebe had sent the wrong pony, Marguerite decided to make the most of the situation. After all, it wasn't the animal's fault. The pony would be fed and tended—and called Misty anyway.

The next morning, the visitor showed a little more life. She gave Marguerite a gentle kick, nothing harsh, just rather playful. Maybe, just maybe, this was Misty after all.

Day after day Misty grew more accustomed to her new home, and especially her new owners. Marguerite never went to the stable without a couple of carrots or a few sugar cubes. Before long Misty was shaking hands and nuzzling under any friendly hand that would groom her coat. The golden sheen returned, and the United States map was white and pure at her lower neck.

Marguerite never went to the barn to visit Misty without taking a carrot or lumps of sugar.

Not only did Misty appreciate life with the Henrys, she also came to life on paper. Each day Marguerite added to her story of a foal making the swim from Assateague Island to Chincoteague Island, and the boy and girl who buy the wild pony. The setting and the characters sounded so real because they were real—all based on the places Marguerite had visited and the people she had met.

Slowly pages became chapters and chapters became a book manuscript. Sidney Henry was a first class critic. Marguerite respected her husband's ideas and opinions. When she finally had a semi-final version of the story written, she gave it to Sidney. Then she tried to busy herself with household duties as he settled into his favorite chair. However, it was impossible to focus on anything but the man she loved most reading the work she loved most. He smiled, frowned, even cried a bit as he flipped the pages. When he finished, Marguerite listened to his every comment. She made changes he suggested, struggling always to make it better. Finally, he said, "Send the book away; now is the time to let go."

Off the manuscript went.

Then came the waiting—that awful time period every writer knows. A day seems like a week. Will the editor like it and want to publish it? Or perhaps will the manuscript be sent back with a match taped to it, suggesting it would be better if it were burned.

Then the news came. Misty of Chincoteague was not only a resident in the stable nearby; *Misty of Chincoteague* was going to be a book.

A quick call went to illustrator Wesley Dennis. As usual, he jumped at the chance to do the book. He had totally enjoyed his visit to Chincoteague, and horses were among his favorite subjects. His collection of photographs filled a cigar box. But when he blocked on a couple drawings, Dennis hurried back to Chincoteague to talk to the Beebe family and make new sketches. The illustrator wanted everything to be just right.

Finally, the book was done. Marguerite pensively awaited publication day. She hoped her reading fans would like it as much as they liked *Justin Morgan Had a Horse*. But maybe that first book had been just a lucky fluke.

Only time—and boys and girls—would decide.

Chapter Five

Horses, Horses, Horses!

Marguerite picked up the telephone. It was her editor at Rand McNally. She listened closely, then set the receiver down. Sidney looked over at her, unable to read her expression.

"I-I guess they think it's going to be a bestseller," Marguerite said, still appearing awestruck. "And the American Library Association has invited Misty to come to their annual convention."

Marguerite's editor was right. From the moment it was published in July of 1947, *Misty of Chincoteague* quickly found its way onto library shelves across the country. Bookstores could not keep it in stock, and boys and girls sat up late at night turning page after page. Rand McNally rewarded Grandpa Beebe with a check for three hundred and fifty dollars for loaning Misty to Marguerite. "We called it an inspiration fee," one of the publishing executives laughed.

Awards and honors flowed in. For the second time, Marguerite won a Newbery Honor Book prize, and it also captured the Lewis Carroll Shelf Award. The Carroll Award signified that *Misty of Chincoteague* ranked alongside the classic *Alice in Wonderland* for its originality and all-around quality. The motion picture studio Twentieth Century picked up an option to make the book into a feature length film. Letters poured into the Henry house. Many contained pictures of horses, of every color and size. The message were usually brief.

Dear Mrs. Henry,

You is my favorate arther. Can I barrow Misty for a while?

Your freind,

Robert

Dear Horse Lady,

I read Misty of Chincoteague ten times. My mother hid the book from me so I would read something else. I found it anyway. Now I am reading it for the eleventh time.

Love,

Linda

Dear Marguerite Henry,

I wish I could write like you. I wish I was Misty and could live with you. When you go back to Chincoteague Island let me know and I will go with you. Please write more stories about horses.

Your best reader,

Paul

Paul could not have known that there was already another horse story whirling around in Marguerite Henry's mind. The idea had come from Wesley Dennis when they were on Chincoteague Island together. The illustrator had mentioned that he had a relative with a book idea. The idea was about a great Godolphin Arabian horse, and Dennis was sure it was just right for Marguerite. What about his relative?

"She'll never do it," Dennis answered. "We'll pay her for the idea, Then we'll do it."

A whole year went by with nothing more being said. Finally, Dennis came to Marguerite and said the story was theirs to do if they wanted it. Once Marguerite heard the idea, she loved it. The story revolved around an Arabian stallion that was born in the stables of the Sultan of Morocco. The sultan sent the pony to Louis XV, the king of France. The king's courtiers made fun of the animal, saying it was weak and sickly compared to the lusty horses in the king's stables. The sultan's gift was cast out to pull carts in Paris. However, the horse eventually became one of three sires in the Thoroughbred line.

Marguerite recognized the gem of a great story, an offshoot of the old Cinderella fairy tale. Giving the tale a working title, *King of the Wind*, words slipped from imagination onto paper.

Before she had barely gotten into her writing, Marguerite ran into obstacles. Her family wanted her

After the publication of Misty of Chincoteague, Marguerite spent hours each day reading letters from readers.

to focus on a story that would not require traveling to other lands and researching another time period. "Not everywhere is safe," they reminded her. After all, *Justin Morgan Had a Horse* and *Misty of Chincoteague* had been runaway bestsellers. Her publishers agreed with Marguerite's family. After looking over her story outline, they talked to her pointedly.

"Are you sure you want to do this book?"

"Yes, of course," Marguerite answered. "Why?"

"Because of your central characters."

"What about them?"

"You have a boy who can't talk."

Marguerite nodded. That was true. Agba, the Moroccan stableboy who would be her main character, was mute. "But sometimes body language can speak louder than words," the writer replied, her voice firmed by conviction.

"And your other characters—the horse and the cat—they can't talk either, except in indecipherable neighs and mews."

"Neighs and mews," Marguerite countered, "can say many things."

"But the settings . . . Morocco, France, England in the eighteenth century! They're so foreign to our good old U.S.A. readers."

There was a long pause. No doubt Marguerite's publishers assumed their prized children's author would suddenly give in. When an author writes for a publisher, that author is said to be "in the publisher's stable," just as Misty was in hers. The publisher hopes for the author to be cooperative, and bended to editorial wishes. Finally, the question came again.

"Are you absolutely sure you want to go ahead with this book? As yet neither you nor Wesley has invested too much time; you could easily turn to a story here at home."

"Too late!" Marguerite declared. "It's like being seven months pregnant. I can't . . . I don't want to do anything but let the seed of the story grow."

That ended the discussion. Marguerite was going to write *King of the Wind*, and that was that.

Once again, Marguerite Henry realized she had been blessed with a special partner—Wesley Dennis. As each chapter of *King of the Wind* came rolling out of her typewriter, the author knew that without Dennis, she never would have had this gem of history that was growing into a magnificent jewel. While her illustrator spurred her imagination with his dramatic action pictures of humans and horses, and different times and places, Marguerite wove facts into fiction. Sham, that grand and glorious stallion, pranced and danced, and flew with the lightning speed of a meteor. Yet Sham, like all of the author's horses, was a horse. Lesser writers created humanlike creatures, but Marguerite Henry never made that mistake. The courage and resourcefulness displayed by each of her horses were within the range of the animal world, true and crisp. To portray them too much like humans would be inaccurate. Worse than that, it would mislead her young readers. "A writer whose audience is young people must write with honesty and care," Marguerite wrote. "There is nothing more precious than a mind forming values, attitudes and knowledge."

With that philosophy in mind and put into practice, Marguerite carved out the story of *King of the Wind*. Once it appeared in 1947, it swept away all the doubts held by her publishers. The faraway countries of Morocco, France and English became close and dear to her young readers. Agba and Sham became special friends, trusted companions on an exciting adventure. "In her book, *King of the Wind*, Marguerite Henry becomes our own Queen of the Children's Horse Story," wrote one reviewer. This time the voters for best children's book of the year could not deny her the honor of the Newbery Award. Despite having runner-up titles for the award with *Justin Morgan Had a Horse* and *Misty of Chincoteague*, Marguerite was shocked — delightfully shocked. Translations of the book went into German, Arabic, Finnish, Persian, Swedish and Italian.

On November 11, 1950, Marguerite Henry stood at a podium to deliver her acceptance speech for the Newbery Award. Members of the American Library Association sat in a hall in Grand Rapids, Michigan, eager to hear what the author had to say.

Misty made a guest appearance at a convention of the American
Library Association.

It had been a long time since Marguerite felt so nervous. The butterflies in her stomach were gigantic, flickering from rib to rib, while her skin raced from hot to cold in seconds. Well, she thought, these people want to know something about the writing of *King of the Wind*. They want to know a bit about me, the author. All I can do is my best.

Marguerite Henry began to speak. First she talked about how she came to write *King of the Wind*. "At first it was nothing but a letterhead. A letterhead and a wish." It had been a journey into the mystery of a faraway land with a different culture. At first it was slow-going, but then the characters took over. "As time went on, some of the characters not only collaborated, they began to do a little bossing."

Marguerite then thanked the many people who had helped her with advice and information in each of her books. Meeting them had added to the joy of writing. She loved every part of the writing and publishing process. "Putting a book to bed—that is, preparing it for the press—is as much fun to me as the writing of it."

Storytelling allowed her to remain a child. "My study is a child's paradise." Pictures of horses and cats and dogs covered the walls. "The child who crosses my threshold gazes in wild delight. It is his dream room come true. It is mine, too."

"I think when a child steps into this little world of mine," she continued, "he subconsciously rips off the pictures I have posted and puts up his own. For an instant this room becomes his. Then often he will look around and say with grave earnestness, 'Will you write a book for me?'"

"I'm a long time answering. How can I tell him that is what I am trying to do. How can I say, 'Johnny, I'm trying! I'm trying to write a book that you can crawl into as snugly as you do your own bed, a book about which you can say, 'This is mine. It fits around me. I fit into it. It fits under and over and around me. It warms me. It is mine, mine, mine!'"

There was a long moment's pause after Marguerite finished speaking. Then, the hall exploded in applause. People rose to their feet, clapping their appreciation. Marguerite sighed deeply, the relief evident in her smile. The butterflies were gone, hiding in shame for the trouble they had caused. Marguerite was smothered between people, librarians singing her praises and wanting to shake her hand.

"You told us so much about the book, but even more importantly about yourself," one woman said.

"Keep writing," another in the crowd gushed. "We have so many Johnny's who need you."

Marguerite nodded. She knew she would keep writing. In fact, she could hardly wait to get home to start a fresh story.

Chapter Six

Enter a Burro

During the early part of her writing career, Marguerite had fussed and worried over every detail on whatever she was doing. If an editor requested a particular manuscript, Marguerite would try to produce it whether she wanted to or not. Sometimes she regretted having accepted an assignment. "That story lacked passion," she told Sidney, "because I really didn't want to write it." Her illustrator, Wesley Dennis, helped Marguerite adopt a new attitude toward her work.

"If it isn't fun, don't do it!" Dennis declared, as if he were delivering the Gettysburg Address. "It's as simple as that."

Dennis practiced what he preached, and gradually Marguerite saw the wisdom of his words. She would listen as an editor shared an idea for a book, or maybe it was a fan or friend. She would think about it, even sleep on it. But what decided whether or not she would do it was Dennis's philosophy: "If it isn't fun, don't do it."

As a writing and illustrating partnership, Marguerite saw Wesley Dennis and herself as very different. He was the "thoroughbred," the courageous one, daring and ready to take chances. He worked swiftly, often having the drawings of a book finished before she had completed the text. She was the "plodding work horse," meticulously searching for every detail to lend authenticity to her work. She was fond of Mark Twain's saying that "The difference between the right word and the almost right word is the difference between lightning and the lighting bug." Marguerite sought just the right word for every sentence. "Young readers deserve the best!" she said often. On paper, she tried to give them just that. In real life, she welcomed the chance to meet her young reading audience. Often that happened at autograph parties. With Wesley Dennis, it was always a special occasion.

"Mrs. Henry, we'd like you to sit here at this table while you autograph your books." The bookstore owner looked around puzzled. "I don't see Mr. Dennis. He was here just a moment ago—"

Without warning, Wesley Dennis appeared from the restroom hallway. He wore a long Sherlock Holmes cap, cradled an unlit ball bellied pipe from his mouth, and carried a giant magnifying glass in his right hand. He approached the store owner, inspected her with the glass, then leaped back. "I say, I say, you are not a child here to get a book autographed, are you? You are one of those pesty creatures known as adults!"

Still perplexed, the bookstore owner turned to Marguerite. "It's all right," the author calmed the woman. "Mr. Dennis is not only a fine illustrator, but he is frustrated actor as well. I shall look after him to see that he does not frighten the children—or the adults!"

Autograph parties gave Marguerite the chance to hear boys and girls respond to her efforts. During the 1940s, women enjoyed wearing hats. Marguerite had a good sense of style with clothing. But she also knew kids. Sometimes she came to autograph parties or library story hours wearing a wild creation on her head. It might be a bouquet of artificial flowers with animals looking out. Or maybe it was it colorful dunce cap!

But Marguerite could never top Wesley Dennis. He was often the biggest—and most childish—guest in attendance. Whether he came dressed as the somber detective Holmes or a laughing face-painted clown, Dennis won applause. The kids loved him, squealing loudly as he drew a miniature sketch of Misty or Sham on their new book frontipiece. Sometimes he even burst into song, attracting even more attention.

But the autograph signings were few compared to the many working sessions between author and illustrator. Their publishers wanted more books with the cash registers cling-clanging record sales, especially

Marguerite and Wesley Dennis loved to go to book signings and meet their readers.

during the holiday seasons. Librarians ordered Henry-Dennis titles sight unseen, knowing that each of their new volumes would bring a new charge of the mite brigade to library checkout counters.

As dedicated as they were to pleasing their publishers, reviewers, and librarians, Marguerite Henry and Wesley Dennis worked hardest to satisfy their reading audience. "If we do not please boys and girls, we work in vain," Marguerite told one magazine reporter.

Book sales for the dynamic Henry-Dennis combination showed that the author and illustrator definitely did NOT work "in vain." They held the top author positions among Rand McNally Publishers.

Marguerite was always on the lookout for a good story idea. She loved to read what other children's authors were producing, but she never copied. It was more fun creating new characters and different storylines of her own. Yet she listened when someone told her about a possible adventure.

When a librarian friend, Mildred Lathrop of Elgin, Illinois, shared a few nuggets of a tale, Marguerite knew at once the story was gold. The yarn had first appeared in *Sunset* magazine, an article telling about a shaggy little burro named Bright Angel. The free and wild creature made his home in the Grand Canyon, enjoying the warm winters on the canyon floor. As summer approached, he headed up the mountainsides to enjoy the company of humans. The guides and rangers in Karibab National Forest welcomed their yearly visitor. The homely burro had no use for work, but he loved sharing a bite to eat with anyone, especially folks with a hearty supply of flapjacks and molasses.

Bright Angel sounded delightful, just the right specimen for a Marguerite Henry story, or at least, she thought so. But as usual, Marguerite had to travel to the source of the action, to soak in the Arizona air, to ride through the Grand Canyon, experiencing up the sights and sounds that Bright Angel knew so well. If there was one ingredient Marguerite Henry demanded for her young readers, it was honesty. She needed to capture the true setting of her action and bring it to life. Yet she did not want to make the trip alone.

Once again Sid Henry agreed to join his wife on another of her journeys. This one was more difficult than others. He hated heights! But he loved seeing his wife excited about a new story. She was like a three-year-old opening a birthday present. He was not about to take away that excitement.

The trip was planned simply enough. Marguerite and Sid hired a guide to take them from the top of the canyon to the bottom, staying overnight at Phantom Ranch on the canyon floor. The next day they would return to the top. The journey would follow the path of Bright Angel. What better way to understand the animal's trip than to travel in his footsteps.

The temperatures dipped below zero as the Henrys prepared for their journey. On the morning of the trip, Sid headed to a small general store to purchase some wooly underwear. The conversation he overheard made him tremble more than the cold February air outside. The store's owner shared the sad tale of two guides who had tried to pass on the canyon trail. The pathway was so narrow, both of the men had fallen to their deaths. It was not the story Sid wanted to hear.

Returning to his room, Sid discovered Marguerite eager to get started. She chuckled when he appeared in his long red woolies. Well, it was Valentine's Day, after all. Why not red underwear?

As they loaded their mules for the descent, the guide handed Marguerite a saddlebag. It was the mail for the people at Phantom Ranch down below. Would she mind keeping it for delivery when they arrived?

Marguerite cheerfully took the saddlebag. Her fears drifted away in the brisk breeze. The mail had to go through. Accepting the delivery job meant she had to reach Phantom Ranch. Clearly, the guide knew what he was doing.

Soon the trio of travelers set off, their mules trudging with sure steps in the frozen snow. Marguerite felt safe, an experienced guide in front of her and her loving husband close behind. Her secure feelings let her think about Bright Angel, the burro who made much the same trip so often. The author's mind absorbed

Marguerite, Sid and a guide on their trip through the Grand Canyon.

each step, each moment, ready to record it on paper later. "Some writers write everything down," she told people. "I think of my mind as a notepad. I am fortunate to have a good memory. My senses are tuned in to whatever I'm doing. I can remember things I see, hear, touch, smell and feel. That helps when I actually sit down to write."

The guide was a perfect match for Marguerite's thinking as they rode. Often the man pointed out rock formations, standing firm and full like pipes of a church organ. Flashes of color spilled from the rock strata. Snow patches sparkled like diamond clusters. The guide was so descriptive that Marguerite hinged on his every word. She turned slightly to catch Sid out of the corner of her eye. He appeared speechless, probably caught up in the radiant beauty of their surroundings. Actually, he was petrified, trying hard not to look down. Never had his acrophobia, that dreaded fear of high places, been so strong. To make matters worse, his mule kept lagging behind, only to suddenly dart forward to catch the others.

Although the three travelers planned to eat a sack lunch they had brought along, no one seemed hungry. The sandwiches and orange went to a pair of stunted deer they encountered as they neared the bottom. A suspension bridge was the final obstacle before arriving at the ranch. By the time they had crossed, Sid's face was whiter than the snow they had trampled along the way.

A feast of wild fowl and rice at Phantom Ranch awaited the travelers. They ate well, but had no strength left—or desire either—for conversation. Marguerite and Sid both slept in their clothes that night— too tired to change.

By early morning, the traveling trio headed back up the canyon. Marguerite welcomed the chance to once again record the sights and sounds in her mind. Yes, now she understood the travels of the burro of whom she planned to write. She had traveled his path, breathed the air and seen the sights.

But that was not enough for Marguerite Henry. She needed more. If she was going to write a real story about a burro, a story her readers could enjoy, more research was needed. She needed to be around a burro, to study and know the animal. Fortunately, such an animal was located easily, only a few miles away from Blackberry Road in Sugar Grove Township. Jiggs, as the animal was called, was immediately renamed Brighty, the name Marguerite had already selected for her star character in her upcoming volume. The burro now found a home in the stable of "Mole Meadows"— the Henry house in Wayne, Illinois. There were three residents in the stable now—Misty, Brighty, and a Morgan colt named Friday. Misty clearly saw herself as being in charge of the place.

Marguerite's method of research was unique. She never outlined a story like so many authors. She kept two sets of manilla folders, each identified by letters written in black crayon. The first set contained story incidents, arranged in order of how they occurred. The second set was filled with facts she gathered about clothing styles, eating habits of the characters, and how they spent their time and money.

To bring her burro character to life, Marguerite watched every move Brighty made. The author saw what the animal ate, how and when he slept, what he liked and disliked. Much of the time Marguerite stayed out of sight, wanting Brighty to behave naturally, unaware of being observed. One thing was certain—the animal could not get enough of carrots and apples! "He is a doctors' dream!" jotted Marguerite, her hand jiggling with laughter.

Finally, Marguerite was ready to write. The story came smoothly, a composite of her journey to Grand Canyon, her observations of Brighty, her outside readings about burros, and all the comments and conversation she had heard since she had focused on what she would be doing. She could hardly wait to see what Wesley Dennis would do with her latest animal friend.

As usual, Dennis worked his own magic with his fingers. No sleek horse this time, no mane blowing in the breeze, no sure-footed stallion prancing and dancing majestically on a sketchpad. Instead, Dennis created a burro, a simple and lovable creature who called the Grand Canyon his home and made the best of the situation.

Marguerite with Brighty and Misty.

The fans of Marguerite Henry and Wesley Dennis greeted *Brighty of the Grand Canyon* with joy and pleasure. "Once again, author Henry takes the reader on an exciting ride, this time with a free spirited four-footed burro named Brighty," wrote one book reviewer. "With the Grand Canyon as a story backdrop, adventure reigns supreme, and when the book is done, the reader knows the canyon is not the only thing "grand" in the book—the writing matches the setting perfectly."

So Brighty quickly joined the special group of four-footed animals hailed as heroes of the young reading set. Visitors came to see the burro, and Misty at times seemed a little annoyed by the fuss made in behalf of a scraggly bunch of wispy hair.

Yet Misty knew who ruled the stable near the little weathered ranch house in Wayne. The pony galloped around the meadow close by, sometimes even giving the family dachshund, Alex, a free ride on her back.

The pony ruled the Henry home as well. When special visitors came and plopped down in the living room for conversation, they were often treated to an appearance by Misty. Always clean—local boys begged to clean and curry any residents of the Henry stable—Misty displayed manners any parents would be proud of. Guests left Mole Meadows with widened eyes, and amazing stories which many listeners doubted.

Grandpa Beebe put this sign on the side of the van sent to take Misty home to Chincoteague.

However, Marguerite knew it was only right to give Misty a chance to fulfill all the possibilities of her animal life. The pony, that wonderful companion at the home in Wayne, needed to go back to Chincoteague, back to where she might mate and produce a colt. Yes, it was time.

Grandpa Beebe sent a van to bring the horse home. The vehicle passed by the wayside church on a Sunday morning, just as the congregation was leaving. A sign on the side of the truck shared the news: MISTY goes home to Chincoteague to have her colt. The driver, Roy Tolbert, thought people should know.

Telephones rang throughout the area that day and night. It wasn't just the Henry's pony, not in the minds of their neighbors. Misty belonged to everyone who knew her. She was a special friend, one that everyone loved.

Early the next morning people started arriving to say their farewells, to pet their friend for a final time, to wish her well and thank her for being such a welcome visitor. Boys and girls begged to be hoisted to give the pony a pat on her nose, her neck, her barrel, and even her rump. Reporters and cameramen from *Life* magazine, UPI news service, the *Chicago Tribune* and others were there too. They asked people for their reactions and wanted folks to explain their tears. One news seeker almost had to run for cover when he said, "After all, it's just a horse." Cameras snapped, the final photo of Misty in the van traveling down the tree-lined road with everyone waving their goodbyes.

Later, that day, Marguerite and Sidney sat quietly, remembering. Suddenly the silence was broken by a loud "Yee-aw, yee-aw, yee-aw-w."

Brighty knew Misty was gone and not coming back. One could hear the sound of a heart breaking in the burro's bray.

Letters from the folks back at Chincoteague lifted the spirits of those Misty had left behind. Grandma Beebe wrote that Grandpa told folks, "I sent a duckling to Illinois and look what I got back. And he says the name Misty like it was made of stars." And then came the news that Misty was with foal, the proud papa being a stallion named Wings, because of his markings.

Then came a fateful April morning when the Henry telephone rang at 5:20 A. M. "It's a boy at Beebe's ranch!" Grandpa declared, not bothering to say hello.

"Misty...? Is she all right?"

"Seems a right proud mother."

"No trouble?"

"No trouble....."

So while the *Life* reporters and the rest of the news media invaded Chincoteague for pictures and stories, the telephone wires around Wayne, Illinois buzzed. "Misty had a boy." There was no need for further identification. Nothing more needed to be said.

Chapter Seven

Riding Into the Sunset

Marguerite's steps were slower now. As she slipped into her 60s, she no longer sought the research that would take her to other countries. Instead, her writing took on a more comfortable mood. The excitement was still there, the action that made boys and girls quickly flip pages, but the settings were closer to home. Always the facts were right, always the details checked and doublechecked. Young readers, librarians and teachers could count on Marguerite Henry to deliver fast moving stories with exact information surrounding them. But the urgency to write, to sit behind a type-writer for hours every day was gone. The pace was slowing.

Gone, too, was Wesley Dennis. The "thoroughbred" of the writer and illustrator team was struck down by a heart attack and died in September of 1966. It was a major loss for Marguerite, who had relied greatly on her co-worker's energy, his enthusiasm and constant good humor. His drawings had always captured in pictures what she had written in words. She did not write for a year. She wondered if she would ever write again. But slowly, ever so slowly, the need to share returned. She began a tale about a wild horse named Annie, and she was on the lookout for an illustrator.

Marguerite came upon a Christmas card painted by Robert Lougheed. The horses featured were just right for her story. At first, Lougheed was totally uninterested. "I'm a gallery painter," he declared, "not a book illustrator." Marguerite smiled. "Fine. Do your paintings gallery size and we'll reduce them for book illustrations. Then you can send your original paintings to galleries." The arrangement worked fine.

Illustrator Lynd Ward specialized in woodcuts. By the time Marguerite met him, he had won a Caldecott Medal, the top award for illustrating a children's book. The author and illustrator were both impressed with each other's attitude toward detail. "You would never find anything in any of Lynd's drawings that was not supposed to be there," Marguerite said. "I liked that because I felt the same way about my stories."

Rich Rudish became one of Marguerite's illustrators by first sending her a fan letter with some of his drawings. She liked them, filing them away in a special folder marked "Promising." Years later, she came upon his work on the covers of top quality horse magazines. When she asked about doing some work for her, he jumped at the chance. Once she saw his efforts, she became his devoted fan.

In 1972, Misty, the horse that belonged to the world, died. She left behind several fine foals, and a number of "grandchildren" as well. Misty had brought joy to thousands, thanks to Marguerite's stories. However, the author was not done with her beloved friend, and she continued to create tales of the filly and its young pals, Mary and Paul Beebe.

Horses had not been the only animals for whom Marguerite shared a special love. Dogs, too, ranked high on her list of favorites. Part of the reason was that Sidney enjoyed them so much. "He never met a canine he didn't love," Marguerite said of her husband. "And the love was returned. Wherever we went, some woebegotten spaniel or terrier trailed after Sid. "It's that way with some people."

As the years turned her hair from amber brown to grey, and the Illinois winters bit deeper into the aging body, the California climate beckoned. Marguerite and Sidney had spent winters in the western warmth, and now they toyed with the idea of making a permanent move. A ranch style homestead in Rancho Santa Fe near San Diego proved irresistable. Too old to care for their own horses, they were close enough to visit neighbors with stables—or just park along the road and watch a proud mare race against the wind.

Awards still rolled in: The Kerlan Award from the University of Minnesota in 1975, and the Illinois Association of English Teachers named her Author of the Diamond Jubilee Year in 1982.

Sidney Henry with a pet dog at their California home.

But the rewards from her writing that she treasured most were the letters that continued to arrive. Scrawled in crayon or typed neatly on bond paper, it did not matter. It was the heartfelt messages that really counted.

Dear Miss Henry,
I know you is old but keep riting. Your books is good.
Sarah Jane

Dear Missus Henry,
I am reading King of the Wind. It is a wonderful book. I took it to bed with me last night and read with a flashlight under the covers. My mom caught me. Please write to her and tell her not to be mad. After all, it was your fault.
Susan

And every now and then, a letter arrived, written in an adult script. Often the message was the same.

Dear Marguerite Henry:
I loved reading you when I was a child. Now, my own children are reading your books and they love them just like I did. Thank you so much for bringing so much joy into so many lives. May you live and write forever!

Mrs. Kathleen Curtis

Sidney was always Marguerite's best reader and critic.

Each note took Marguerite back to her typewriter, eager to create another story. After all, there were readers to please—readers who deserved the best.

In 1987, Marguerite lost her biggest fan. The death of Sidney Crocker Henry took from her life a husband of sixty-four years. Biologically, they had had no children. Yet, together, they had shared a pony, a burro, three fox cubs, a horse, a dachshund, and a mom-cat who never stopped having kittens. Scared to death of heights, he had ridden the Grand Canyon with her, read her first drafts of manuscripts, adding commas and insight. It would be a lonelier world without him. Yet it was the words of Grandma Beebe who brought a special comfort to Marguerite. "No one ever dies, not a person or a single pony. Nothing dies as long as there is the memory to enfold it and a heart to love it."

After Sidney's death, Marguerite continued to write. But the words came slower now, and as she entered her nineties, a series of strokes weakened both her mind and body. When she died on November 26, 1997, she was working on a story about her poodle, Patrick Henry, who was by her side.

"She never lost that wonderful, exuberant, childlike quality," said Susan Foster Ambrose, a close friend and fellow writer. "She would be fascinated with a sunset or a bird landing in her back yard. She was just so captivated by the small joys in her life, and she was able to translate the small joys to her readers."

Through her books, she still does.

Appendix

Marguerite Henry's
Newbery Acceptance Speech

"*King of the Wind* was a long time growing. At first it was nothing but a letterhead. A letterhead and a wish.

"Cupped in a fertile valley at the foot of the Blue Ridge Mountains is a vast breeding ground for thoroughbreds. Several years ago the owner, Walter Chrysler, wanted the head of the Godolphin Arabian engraved on his stationery; for it was the blood of this famous horse that had flowed down the centuries to give speed and stamina to the stallions and bloodmares in Mr. Chrysler's stable. So proud was he of this heritage that he engaged the artist, Wesley Dennis, to draw a faithful likeness of the head. The artist sent his assistant to the library to find in old books an accurate portrayal. As the Godolphin Arabian was foaled in 1724 there were, of course, no photographs of him but only artists' likenesses. It was not the drawings of the little horse with the extraordinary crest that intrigued the assistant, however; it was the fact that all through his life no one had foreseen any greatness in him!

Overworked and underfed, he drew a wood cart in the streets of Paris. Yet in spite of his degrading experiences and menial tasks, no one could quench the fire in his veins. He lived to become one of the greatest foundation sires of the thoroughbred line.

"The assistant wanted to write the Godolphin story, and for years Wesley waited to do the illustrations, while the excitement grew within him. 'If only I could tell you about another horse of history!' he would say while we were putting the book of Justin Morgan together. And I would reply with quick imploring, 'Don't! I can't trust myself to know about it if someone else is at work on the idea.' But the hints were like nettles.

The story of Little Bub was completed; and before the sound of his hoofbeats had dimmed, I was lost in the wilds of Pennsylvania with a Quaker lad named Benjamin West. Then pony Misty was foaled and her story, too, was finished. At last Wesley's assistant decided it was unlikely she would ever find time to write the Godolphin story; so Wesley was free to talk about it.

"With great excitement I began to probe and pry into the life of this famous stallion who had rubbed shoulders with sultans and kings, with cooks and carters. Here were no burned-out cinders of history. Here were live coals showering their sparks over Morocco, France, England.

"Sultan Mulai Ismael of Morocco, the stableboy Agba, the blackhearted wood carter, Quaker Coke of London, the Keeper of the Red Lion, the Earl of Godolphin—here were real characters. And Roxana, Hobgoblin, Regulus, Cade, Lath were real horses. Little by little and quite of their own volition they began to collaborate with me, to take me into their confidence.

"I began to see the Earl of Godolphin not just as an aristocrat who owned a stable of pleasure horses. His passion was horses, blooded horses. He longed to improve the English strain. I felt the fear in him, the secret fear that just when he was on the eve of creating a new breed of horses his money was running out faster than sands in an hourglass.

"And Jethro Coke made it plain that it was from pity he bought the little horse from between the shafts of the wood cart, not because he saw any greatness in them.

"As time went on, some of the characters were not only collaborated they began to do a little bossing. Certain things were inevitable, and they made me see this. For example, I thought I was arguing with myself that Agba could not be a mute. Children might be repelled. But all the time Agba's dark burning eyes, his thin hands, his shoulders were talking to me more articulately than any words. It was he who made the decision.

"To put myself into the long ago and far away I peppered my study walls with photostats. There were Arabian boys in their hooded mantles; sultans swaying along on their horses with wondrous fringed parasols held over them; wood carters snaking bullwhips over little cobs drawing big-wheeled carts; foppish French nobles admiring their curls in a beauty salon where wigs were pegged on the walls like scalps. And there were English scenes of thatched-roof cottages, of kitchens with hares and partridges dangling from the rafters like furry swords of Danocles, of Newmarket at the height of a royal race meeting.

"There were pictures of actual characters such as the Earl of Godolphin, magnificent in his cascade of white ruffles; Sultan Mulai Ismael the Fat, sitting on his dais; the boy king, Louis XV, riding his stout horse; George II of England, strutting big to make up for his littleness; Queen Caroline, tall as a pikestaff, followed by her stepping-stone daughters in their little weird hoods.

"Suddenly, I was no longer hemmed in by study walls. I had leaped over the years. I was Agba flying through the streets of Meknes. I was Sham struggling to keep my footing on icy cobblestones. I was the Godophin Arabian being crowned with royal plumes from the Queen's own headdress.

"It was the present that grew dim and the long ago that became real! Even at noon when I set aside my work and went to the barn to water Misty and Friday, I was still in the past. It was not Misty's blond eyelashes that brushed against my hand as I held her water bucket, but those of Sham, the fleet one.

"Present-day people helped play the little game with me. There was Samuel W. Riddle, owner of Man O'War. It was his beloved Big Red that helped to fasten draw-chains on the past. If I could make children understand that this hero of theirs was a direct descendant of the Godolphin Arabian, history would no longer sleep with closed, waxen eyelids; it would quicken to life.

"Old press notices said that Man O'War was retired because of a bowed tendon, and checking on this statement brought me my cherished friendship with Mr. Riddle. I sent my opening chapter on Man O'War to him and he replied as follows:

Dear Mrs. Henry:

I liked your Morgan story, but I was shocked at what you wrote about Man O'War. He retired to the stud without a mark on him, never broke down or had a bowed tendon. Whoever told you this is a word of four letters beginning with L. I retired him as a three-year-old because his handicapper told me he would give him more weight than ever a horse carried as a four-year-old.

I will be eighty-seven years old next July and I have tried to tell the truth all my life. Now I am too old to change. If you want to know anything more about Man O'War, come and see me.

Very sincerely,
S. D. Riddle

"As the letter with its Florida address arrived in the dead of a typical Chicago winter, who could refuse so tempting an invitation?

"I did go to Florida and there wrote and re-wrote the chapter. On the day I took it to Mr. Riddle, I found him sitting with his back to the sun and the sea. His eyes were the blueness of the sea and his hair the whiteness of the breakers. When I finished reading to him about his immortal Man O'War, I looked up to find a tear spilling down his cheek. Then I cried too, and we were friends. The rest of the day we spent at his stable at Hialeah, where I met more descendants of the Godolphin Arabian than a body can dream of.

"Always there seems to be a gentle man with blue eyes and whitened hair who lends encouragement and faith to my stories. For *Misty* there was the inimitable Grandpa Beebe with his salty philosophy. It was he who dealt such wisdom as 'Facts are fine, fer as they go, but they're like water bugs skittering atop the water. Legends, now—they go deep down and bring up the heart of a story.'

"With *Justin Morgan* it was David Dana Hewitt. He was 98 years old but young enough to ride my questions with a loose rein. In his fine, steady handwriting he made me see Vermont. Not the Vermont that greets you with paved highways, but the Vermont that lies deep in the soul of its people.

"For *King of the Wind* querying letters went out by the basketful, to librarians and historians, to horsemen and Quakers. From Mary Alice Lamb, birthright Quaker and authority of early Quaker history, I learned my English 'thee's and "thou's' as known, that the plural forms of 'thee' and 'thy' are 'you' and 'your.' She agreed that 'you' did sound un-Quakerish, but that was the way of it.

"From Joachim Wach, Professor of Comparative Religion, I learned the Mohammedans believe in heaven, that in their Koran are many references to the 'garden' and the happiness of those dwelling there. And so when Agba and Sham and Grimalkin were on the highroad to Gog Magog, I found myself saying, 'If the road to the hills of Gog Magog had been the road to heaven, the three silent creatures could not have been less happier.' I'd write a whole horse van of letters for little nuggets like this.

"In planning a book I like to think it out in scenes and I am always astounded that they cannot hang in mid-air. I'm in such a state of eagerness to get on to the next big scene that I forget there must be bridges between them. Children need them for security. Often little catwalks will do.

"These bridges have always been my big problem. On the manuscript describing the scene in *Justin Morgan* where Joel Goss enlisted in the War of 1812, Helen Ferris of the Junior Literary Guild noted:

'Danger! Bridge out! Don't you think disposing of the War in 1812 in a sentence and a half is a little abrupt?'

"Her warning led me on one of my most exciting quests. I attacked the war from the viewpoint of the doctors and veterinarians. The next thing I knew I was in the heat of battle in Lundy's Lane, thrusting muskets in sleeves to make litters for the wounded men, then going to the horses, pouring alum in their wounds, quieting their screaming. And so what was once a gossamer thread became strong enough for hobnailed boots.

"One would think I might have learned about transitions for this experience. But no. In *King of the Wind* I hopscotched from continent to continent with thoughtless abandon. Signor Achmet with his stallions and horseboys board ship at Tangier. The horses are sleek, their haunches gleam satin in the sun. In the next scene in Versailles they are bags of bones. This is where I need help and it comes in the form of a pertinent question by Dr. Mary Alice Jones, my editor, 'What happened to make them thin?'

"Then, quite gallantly, the blackguard of a captain prompts me in a stage whisper. With a sly wink and a twirl of his moustaches, he admits to pocketing the money for oats and feeding the horses on nothing but straw.

"Subconsciously I felt that my editor might find the triangle scene between the stallions, Hobgoblin and

Sham, and the mare, Lady Roxana, distasteful to gentle readers. Imagine my surprise and delight when she wrote in the margin of an early draft, 'Doesn't this happen too fast? Should there be more time for love-making?' Never was a suggestion accepted more joyously!

"Wesley, too, must have been restrained by the same inhibitions, for when his picture of Newgate Prison came in, the comment in the editorial and art offices was, 'Too pleasant. Looks like a library instead of a jail.' With obvious glee Wesley lengthened and sharpened the spikes on the overgate until all comparisons to a library were hewn away!

"Putting a book to bed—that is, preparing it for the press—is as much fun to me as the writing of it. It provides the excitement of playing in an orchestra, with none of the dull hours of practicing. I can't play a note of music because as a child I felt that a pin in the doorbell of a Saturday morning was a good way to keep the music teacher out, but I still feel a lot of music inside me. Happily the art department at Rand McNally actually encourages me to come in and blow my little oboe of ideas.

"The visual properties of a book, the tactile qualities—picture layout, size and kind of type, the cloth for the cover, the stamping—are as deeply important to me as the context. Working with all departments is akin in my mind to playing in a great orchestra. The tumult and triumph and cymbals and swells of sound are all there. So too is the sense of belonging, not as a solo player, but as part of the whole! The ectasy of belonging! It must be the same feeling that horses have when they switch tails for each other in flying-squirrels!

"At home I still have this sense of belonging because of the children who come to help me on my new books. My tiny study is a child's paradise. The walls are covered with pictures—our silky-haired spaniel at a tender age; two cats, Pinky Nose and Tim, who are teasing to be put into a story; a boy and a girl going up in a swing. And horses! Horses walking, horses trotting, horses galloping, horses blown, horses in repose, colts frisking, foals sucking.

"The child who crosses my threshold gazes in wild delight. It is his dream room come true. It is mine, too. Perhaps his childhood room is not unlike the one I remember with walls painted fresh and clean and not to be desecrated with a motley collecting of disarming animals with liquid, questing eyes.

"I think when a child steps into this little world of mine he subconsciously rips off the pictures I have posted and puts up his own. For an instant this room becomes his. Then often he will look around and say with grave earnestness, 'Will you write a book for me? Not for any other boy. Just for me?'

"I'm a long time answering. How can I tell him that is what I am trying to do? How can I say, 'Johnny, I'm trying! I'm trying to write a book that you can crawl into as snugly as you do into your own bed, a book about which you can say, 'This is mine. It fits around me. I fit into it. It fits under and over and around me. It warms me. It is mine, mine, mine!'

"Haltingly, I do say, 'Johnny, books aren't just one-sided. It takes an understanding reader to discover his own book. The writer is no more than the farmer with his bag of seeds. The reader is a field, new plowed in spring. The farmer scatters his seeds, but all the plants that grow from them do not come up alike. Some are small and spindling and some are big and strong. That's the way it is with books. Sometimes a book gives you a small moment of happiness, and sometimes when you close the cover, the book grows big within you, like a boll of cotton bursting its seams. Someday, Johnny, I hope you'll say to me, 'This book you wrote for me.'

"It is children like Johnny who make me loath to give up a manuscript. In fact, if it weren't for deadlines I'd still be working on *King of the Wind*. The doing is so much more fun than the getting through. The only really dismal days in my life are those when I turn in a manuscript. I am suddenly bereft. It is as if the sun had slid into the horizon and a cold curtain of rain had slapped across my face. A whole lifetime of emptiness seems to stretch out before me.

"And then, oh happy relief! In a little while the manuscript is back home, with blessed little question marks along the margins. Then once again, I'm happy. I've got work to do! The editor's in her chair; all's right with the world.

"Now this book is finished. Sham has been crowned, and in the crowing Agba too has been honored. As custodian for them I accept the Newbery Medal. It is the shininess of Sham's coat in the sun. It is the color, too, of the slim brown horseboy who loved him. In their honor I will keep it shining always."

Awards and Honors

JUSTIN MORGAN HAD A HORSE
Newbery Honor Book (1946)
Junior Scholastic Gold Seal Award (1948)
Award of the Friends of Literature (1948)

MISTY OF CHINCOTEAGUE
Newbery Honor Book (1948)
Lewis Carroll Shelf Award (1961)

KING OF THE WIND
Newbery Medal (1949)
Young Readers Choice Award (1951)

SEA STAR: ORPHAN OF CHINCOTEAGUE
Young Readers Choice Award (1952)

BRIGHTY OF THE GRAND CANYON
William Allen White Award (1956)

BLACK GOLD
Sequoyah Children's Book Award (1960)

MUSTANG, WILD SPIRIT OF THE WEST
Sequoyah Children's Book Award (1970)
Western Heritage Award (1967)

GAUDENZIA: PRIDE OF THE PALIO
Children's Reading Round Table Award (1961)
Society of Midland Authors Clara Ingram
Judson Award (1961)

SAN DOMINGO: THE MEDICINE
HAT STALLION
Society of Midland Authors Clara Ingram
Judson Award (1973)
Literature for Children Award - Southern
   California Council (1973)
Kerlan Award - University of Minnesota (1975)
Author of the Diamond Jubilee Year -
   Illinois Association Teachers of English (1982)
Honorary Doctor of Letters - Hamilton College (1992)

Bibliography

Henry, Marguerite. *Dear Readers and Riders,*
   Chicago: Rand McNally, 1969.
---. *The Illustrated Marguerite Henry*,
   Chicago: Rand McNally, 1980.
---. *Marguerite Henry: Something About the Author
   Autobiography Series*, Volume 7, Detroit:Gale
   Research Company, 1989, 91-108.
---. "Newbery Acceptance Paper." Boston: *The Horn
Book*. January-February, 1950, 9-17.
---. *A Pictorial Life History of Misty*.
   Chicago: Rand McNally, 1976.
"Henry, Marguerite." *Children's Literature
   Review* - Volume 4, Detroit: Gale
   Research Company, 1982, 104-116.
"Henry, Marguerite." *Twentieth-Century Children's
   Writers*, Third Edition, New York: St. James Press,
   1989, 443-444.

Jupp, Gertrude B. *"My Little Sister Marguerite Henry." The Horn Book.* January-February, 1940, 18-24.

Lukens, Rebecca," Marguerite Henry." *Dictionary of Literary Biography:American Writers for Children 1900-1960* —Volume 22, Detroit: Gale Research Company, 1983, 217-222.

Mooar, Brian, *"Kids' Author Marguerite Henry Dies."* Chicago: *Chicago Sun-Times*, November 28, 1997, 3.

Saxon, Wolfgang. "Marguerite Henry, 95, Author of the 'Chincoteague' Series." *New York Times*, November 29, 1997, A13.

Smaridge, Norah. *Famous Modern Storytellers for Young People*. New York: Dodd Mead & Company, 1969, 98-104.

Wilt, Miriam E. *"In Marguerite Henry—The Thread That Runs So True." Elementary English*, November, 1954, 387-395.

Major Works

Auno and Tauno: A Story of Finland (illustrated by
   Gladys Blackwood). Chicago: Albert Whitman,
   1940.
Dilly Dally Sally (illustrated by G. Blackwood). Akron,
   Ohio: Saalfield, 1940.
Geraldine Belinda (illustrated by G. Blackwood). New
   York: Platt & Munk, 1942.
Their First Igloo on Baffin Island, with Barbara True (illus-
   trated by G. Blackwood). Chicago: Albert Whitman,
   1943; London: Gifford, 1945.
A Boy and a Dog (illustrated by Diana Thorne and Ottilie
   Foy). Chicago: Wilcox & Follett, 1944.
Justin Morgan Had a Horse (illustrated by Wesley Dennis).
   Chicago: Wilcox & Follett, 1945.
The Little Fellow. (illustrated by D. Thorne). Philadelphia:
   Winston, 1945; (illustrated by Rich Rudish). Chicago:
   Rand McNally, 1975.
Robert Fulton, Boy Craftsman (illustrated by Lawrence
   Dresser). Indianapolis: Bobbs-Merrill, 1945.
Misty of Chincoteague (illustrated by W. Dennis). Chicago:
   Rand McNally, 1947; London: Collins, 1961.

Always Reddy (illustratedby W. Dennis). New York
  and London: McGraw Hill, 1947.
Benjamin West and His Cat Grimalkin (illustrated by
  W. Dennis). Indianapolis: Bobbs-Merrill, 1947.
King of the Wind (illustrated by Wesley Dennis). Chicago:
  Rand McNally, 1948; London: Constable, 1957.
Little-or-Nothing from Nottingham (illustrated by W.
  Dennis). New York: McGraw Hill, 1949.
Sea Star, Orphan of Chincoteague (illustrated by W.
  Dennis). Chicago: Rand McNally, 1949; London:
  Collins, 1968.
Born to Trot (illustrated by W. Dennis). Chicago: Rand
  McNally, 1950; excerpts published as *One Man's Horse*.
  Chicago: Rand McNally, 1977.
Brighty of the Grand Canyon (illustrated by W.
  Dennis). Chicago: Rand McNally, 1953; London:
  Collins, 1970.
Cinnabar, the One O'Clock Fox (illustrated by W.
  Dennis). Chicago: Rand McNally, 1956.
Misty, the Wonder Pony, by Misty, Herself (illustrated by
  Clare McKinley). Chicago: Rand McNally, 1956.
Black Gold (illustrated by W. Dennis). Chicago: Rand
  McNally, 1957.
Muley-Ears, Nobody's Dog (illustrated by W. Dennis).
  Chicago: Rand McNally, 1959.
Gaudenzia, Pride of the Palio (illustrated by Lynd Ward).
  Chicago: Rand McNally, 1960; London: Collins, 1971.
Five O'Clock Charlie (illustrated by W. Dennis).
  Chicago: Rand McNally, 1962; London: Collins, 1963.
Stormy, Misty's Foal (illustrated by W. Dennis).
  Chicago: Rand McNally, 1963; London: Collins, 1965.

White Stallion of Lipizza (illustrated by W. Dennis).
Chicago: Rand McNally, 1964; London: Blackie, 1976.

Mustang, Wild Spirit of the West (illustrated by Robert
Lougheed). Chicago: Rand McNally, 1966; London:
Collins, 1968.

Stories from Around the World. Chicago: Hubbard Press,
1971.

San Domingo: The Medicine Hat Stallion (illustrated by
R. Lougheed). Chicago: Rand McNally, 1972.

*Marguerite Henry's Misty Treasury: The Complete Misty,
Sea Star, and Story* (illustrated by W. Dennis). Chicago:
Rand McNally, 1982.

Our First Pony (illustrated by R. Rudish). Chicago: Rand
McNally, 1984.

Index

Reader's Digest, 40
Roosevelt, Alice, 10
Roosevelt, Ethel, 10
Roosevelt, Theodore, 12
Rudish, Rich, 85

Saturday Evening Post, The,
    38, 40
Shakespeare, William, 21, 28
Sherman, James, 12-13
Sunset Magazine, 72

Tolbert, Roy, 82
Twain, Mark, 18, 69
Twentieth Century, 59

Ward, Lynn, 85

I was dreaming when you woke me up? I dreamt dat you shook your old rusty black fist under my nose and I split your head open wid a axe.' Then she'll kick your feets away from hers, snatch de covers all over on her side, ball up her fists agin, and gwan back to sleep. You can't tell me nothing. I know." "My people!"

This always was, and is still, good for a raucous burst of laughter. I listened to this talk and became more and more confused. If it was so honorable and glorious to be black, why was it the yellow-skinned people among us had so much prestige? Even a child in the first grade could see that this was so from what happened in the classroom and on school programs. The light-skinned children were always the angels, fairies and queens of school plays. The lighter the girl, the more money and prestige she was apt to marry. So on into high school years, I was asking myself questions. Were Negroes the great heroes I heard about from the platform, or were they the ridiculous monkeys of every-day talk? Was it really honorable to be black? There was even talk that it was no use for Negro boys and girls to rub all the hair off of their heads against college walls. There was no place for them to go with it after they got all this education. Some of the older heads held that it was too much for Negroes to handle. Better leave such things for the white folks, who knew what to do with it. But there were others who were all for pushing ahead. I saw the conflict in my own home between my parents. My mother was the one to dare all. My father was satisfied.

This Negro business came home to me in incidents and ways. There was the time when Old Man Bronner was taken out and beaten. Mr. Bronner was a white man of the poor class who had settled in aristocratic Maitland. One night just after dark, we heard terrible cries back in the woods behind Park Lake. Sam Mosely, his brother Elijah, and Ike Clarke, hurried up to our gate and they were armed. The howls of pain kept up. Old fears and memories must have stirred inside of the grown folks. Many people closed and barred their doors. Papa

185

and the men around our gate were sullen and restless as the cries churned over the woods and lake.

"Who do you reckon it is?" Sam Mosely asked.

"I don't know for sure, but some thinks it's Jim Watson. Anyhow, he ain't home yet," Clarke said, and all of them looked at each other in an asking way.

Finally Papa said, "Well, hold on a minute till I go get my rifle."

"Tain't no ifs and buts about it," Elijah Mosely said gravely. "We can't leave Jim Watson be beat to death like that."

Papa had sensed that these armed men had not come to merely stand around and talk. They had come to see if he would go with the rest. When he came out shoving the sixteen bullets into his rifle, and dropping more into his pocket, Mama made no move to stop him. "Well, we all got families," he said with an attempt at lightness. "Shoot off your gun, somebody, so de rest will know we ready."

Papa himself pointed his Winchester rifle at the sky and fired a shot. Another shot answered him from around the store and a huddle of figures came hurrying up the road in the dark.

"It's Jim Watson. Us got to go git him!" and the dozen or more men armed with double-barreled shotguns, breech-loaders, pistols and Papa's repeating Winchester hurried off on their grim mission. Perhaps not a single one of them expected to return alive. No doubt they hoped. But they went.

Mama gasped a short sentence of some sort and herded us all into the house and barred the door. Lights went out all over the village and doors were barred. Axes had been dragged in from wood piles, grass-hooks, pitch-forks and scythes were ranked up in corners behind those barred doors. If the men did not come back, or if they only came back in part, the women and children were ready to do the best they could. Mama spoke only to say she wished Hezekiah and John, the two biggest boys, had not gone to Maitland late in the afternoon. They were not back and she feared they might start home and— But she did not cry. Our seven hounds with big, ferocious Ned in the lead, barked around the house. We huddled around Mama in her room and kept quiet. There was not a human sound in all the village. Nothing had ever happened before in our vicinity to create such tension. But people had memories and told tales of what happened back there in Georgia, and Alabama and West Florida that made the skin of the young crawl with transmitted memory, and reminded the old heads that they were still flinchy.

The dark silence of the village kept up for an hour or more. The once loud cries fell and fell until our straining ears could no longer find them. Strangest of all, not a shot was fired. We huddled in the dark and waited, and died a little, and waited. The silence was ten times more punishing than the cries.

At long last, a bubble of laughing voices approached our barn from the rear. It got louder and took on other dimensions between the barn and the house. Mama hissed at us to shut up when, in fact, nobody was saying a thing.

"Hey, there Little-Bits," Papa bellowed. "Open up!"

"Strike a light, Daught," Mama told my sister, feeling around in the dark to find Sarah's hand to give her the matches which I had seen clutched in her fingers before she had put out the light. Mama had said very little, and I could not see her face in the dark; somehow she could not scratch a match now that Papa was home again.

All of the men came in behind Papa, laughing and joking, perhaps more from relief than anything else.

"Don't stand there grinning like a chessy cat, Mr. Hurston," Mama scolded. "You ain't told me a thing."

"Oh, it wasn't Jim Watson at all, Lulu. You remember 'bout a week ago Old Man Bronner wrote something in de Orlando paper about H.'s daughter and W.B.J.'s son being seen sitting around the lakes an awful lot?"

"Yeah, I heard something about it."

"Well, you know those rich white folks wasn't going to 'low nothing like dat. So some of 'em waylaid him this evening. They pulled him down off of a load of hay he was hauling and drug him off back there in de woods and tanned his hide for him."

"Did y'all see any of it?"

"Nope, we could hear him hollering for a while, though. We never got no further than the lake. A white man, one of the J—— boys was standing in the bushes at de road. When we got ready to turn off round de lake he stepped out and spoke to us and told us it didn't concern us. They had Bronner down there tied down on his all-fours, and de men was taking turns wid dat bull whip. They must have been standing on tip-toes to do it. You could hear them licks clear out to de road."

The men all laughed. Somebody mocked Bronner's cries and moans a time or two and the crowd laughed immoderately. They had gone out to rescue a neighbor or die in the attempt, and they were back with their families. So they let loose their insides and laughed. They resurrected a joke or two and worried it like a bone and laughed some more. Then they just laughed. The men who spoke of members of their race as monkeys had gone out to die for one. The men who were always saying, "My skin-folks, but not kinfolks; my race but not my taste," had rushed forth to die for one of these same contemptibles. They shoved each other around and laughed. So I could see that what looked like ridicule was really the Negro poking a little fun at himself. At the same time, just like other people, hoping and wishing he was what the orators said he was.

My mother eased back in her chair and took a dip of snuff. Maybe she did not feel so well, for she didn't get tickled at all. After a while, she ordered us off to bed in a rough voice. Time was, and the men scattered. Mama sat right where she was until Hezekiah and John came home around ten o'clock. She gave them an awful going over with her tongue for staying out late, and then she eased to bed.

I was dredged up inside that night, so I did not think about the incident's general connection with race. Besides I had to go to sleep. But days later, it was called to my recollection again. There was a program at the Methodist Church, and Mrs. Mattie Moseley, it was announced, was to have a paper.

She was also going to have a fine new dress to read it in. We all wanted to see the dress.

The time came and she had the dress on. The subject of her paper was, "What will the Negroes do with the Whites?" I do not know what she decided was to be done. It seemed equally unimportant to the rest of the town. I remember that everybody said it was a fine subject. But the next week, the women talked about nothing else but the new wrist watch she had on. It was the first one ever seen in our town.

But in me, the affair stirred up more confusion. Why bring the subject up? Something was moving around me which I had no hooks to grasp. What was this about white and black people that was being talked about?

Certainly nothing changed in the village. The townspeople who were in domestic service over in Maitland or Winter Park went to work as usual. The white people interested in Eatonville came and went as before. Mr. Irving Batchellor, the author, who had a show place in Winter Park, petted up Willie Sewell, who was his head gardener, in the same old way. Bishop Whipple petted Elijah Mosely, and Mrs. Mars, who was his sister, did lots of things for Lulu Mosely, Elijah's wife. What was all the talk about? It certainly was puzzling to me.

As time went on, the confusion grew. By the time that I got to high school, I was conscious of a group that was neither the top nor the bottom of Negrodom. I met the type which designates itself as "the better-thinking Negro." I was thrown off my stride by finding that while they considered themselves Race Champions, they wanted nothing to do with anything frankly Negroid. They drew color lines within the race. The Spirituals, the Blues, *any* definitely Negroid thing was just not done. They went to the trouble at times to protest the use of them by Negro artists. Booker T. Washington was absolutely vile for advocating industrial education. There was no analysis, no seeking for merits. If it was old Cuffy, down with it! "My People! My People!"

This irritated me until I got to the place where I could analyze. The thing they were trying to do went wrong because it lacked reason. It lacked reason because they were attempting to stand equal with the best in America without having the tools to work with. They were attempting a flight away from Negro-dom because they felt that there was so much scorn for black skin in the nation that their only security was in flight. They lacked the happy carelessness of a class beneath them and the understanding of the top-flight Negro above them. Once, when they used to set their mouths in what they thought was the Boston Crimp, and ask me about the great differences between the ordinary Negro and "the better-thinking Negro," I used to show my irritation by saying I did not know who the better-thinking Negro was. I knew who the think-they-are-better Negroes were, but who were the better-thinkers was another matter. But when I came to understand what made them make their useless motions, and saw them pacing a cage that wasn't there, I felt more sympathy than irritation. If they want to establish a sort of fur-coat peerage, let 'em! Since they can find no comfort where they happened to be born, no especial talents to lift them, and other doors are closed to them, they have to find some pleasure somewhere in life. They have to use whatever their mentality provides. "My People! My People!"

So I sensed early, that the Negro race was not one band of heavenly love. There was stress and strain inside as well as out. Being black was not enough. It took more than a community of skin color to make your love come down on you. That was the beginning of my peace.

But one thing and another kept the conflict going on inside me, off and on for years. Sometimes I was sure that the Negro race was all that the platform speakers said. Then I would hear so much self-deprecation that I would be deflated. Over and over I heard people shake their heads and explain us by the supposed prayer of a humble Negro, who got down on his knees and said: "Lawd, you know I ain't nothing. My wife, she ain't nothing. My chillun ain't nothing, and if you fool 'round us, Lawd, you won't be nothing neither."

Light came to me when I realized that I did not have to

consider any racial group as a whole. God made them duck by duck and that was the only way I could see them. I learned that skins were no measure of what was inside people. So none of the Race clichés meant anything anymore. I began to laugh at both white and black who claimed special blessings on the basis of race. Therefore I saw no curse in being black, nor no extra flavor by being white. I saw no benefit in excusing my looks by claiming to be half Indian. In fact, I boast that I am the only Negro in the United States whose grandfather on the mother's side was *not* an Indian chief. Neither did I descend from George Washington, Thomas Jefferson, nor any Governor of a Southern state. I see no need to manufacture me a legend to beat the facts. I do not coyly admit to a touch of the tarbrush to my Indian and white ancestry. You can consider me Old Tar-Brush in person if you want to. I am a mixed-blood, it is true, but I differ from the party line in that I neither consider it an honor nor a shame. I neither claim Jefferson as my grandpa, nor exclaim, "Just look how that white man took advantage of my grandma!" It does not matter in the first place, and then in the next place, I do not know how it came about. Since nobody ever told me, I give my ancestress the benefit of the doubt. She probably ran away from him just as fast as she could. But if that white man could run faster than my grandma, that was no fault of hers. Anyway, you must remember, he didn't have a thing to do but to keep on running forward. She, being the pursued, had to look back over her shoulder every now and then to see how she was doing. And you know your ownself, how looking backwards slows people up.

In this same connection, I have been told that God meant for all the so-called races of the world to stay just as they are, and the people who say that may be right. But it is a well known fact that no matter where two sets of people come together, there are bound to be some in-betweens. It looks like the command was given to people's heads, because the other parts don't seem to have heard tell. When the next batch is made up, maybe Old Maker will straighten all that out.

191

Maybe the men will be more tangle-footed and the women a whole lot more faster around the feet. That will bring about a great deal more of racial and other kinds of purity, but a somewhat less exciting world. It might work, but I doubt it. There will have to be something harder to get across than an ocean to keep East and West from meeting. But maybe Old Maker will have a remedy. Maybe even He has given up. Perhaps in a moment of discouragement He turned the job over to Adolf Hitler and went on about His business of making more beetles.

I do not share the gloomy thought that Negroes in America are doomed to be stomped out bodaciously, nor even shackled to the bottom of things. Of course some of them will be tromped out, and some will always be at the bottom, keeping company with other bottom-folks. It would be against all nature for all the Negroes to be either at the bottom, top, or in between. It has never happened with anybody else, so why with us? No, we will go where the internal drive carries us like everybody else. It is up to the individual. If you haven't got it, you can't show it. If you have got it, you can't hide it. That is one of the strongest laws God ever made.

I maintain that I have been a Negro three times—a Negro baby, a Negro girl and a Negro woman. Still, if you have received no clear cut impression of what the Negro in America is like, then you are in the same place with me. There is no *The Negro* here. Our lives are so diversified, internal attitudes so varied, appearances and capabilities so different, that there is no possible classification so catholic that it will cover us all, except My people! My people!

CHAPTER 13

TWO WOMEN IN PARTICULAR

Two women, among the number whom I have known intimately force me to keep them well in mind. Both of them have rare talents, are drenched in human gravy, and both of them have meant a great deal to me in friendship and inward experience. One, Fanny Hurst because she is so young for her years, and Ethel Waters because she is both so old and so young for hers.

Understand me, their ages have nothing to do with their birthdays. Ethel Waters is still a young woman. Fanny Hurst is far from old.

In my undergraduate days I was secretary to Fanny Hurst. From day to day she amazed me with her moods. Immediately before and after a very serious moment you could just see her playing with her dolls. You never knew where her impishness would break out again.

One day, for instance, I caught her playing at keeping house with company coming to see her. She told me not to leave the office. If the doorbell rang, Clara, her cook, was to answer it. Then she went downstairs and told Clara that I was to answer the doorbell. Then she went on to another part of the house.

Presently I heard the bell, and it just happened that I was on my way downstairs to get a drink of water. I wondered why Clara did not go to the door. What was my amazement to see Miss Hurst herself open the door and come in, greet herself graciously and invite herself to have some tea. Which she did. She went into that huge duplex studio and had toasted English muffins and played she had company with her for an hour or more. Then she came on back up to her office and went to work.

I knew that she was an only child. She did not even have cousins to play with. She was born to wealth. With the help of images, I could see that lonely child in a big house making up her own games. Being of artistic bent, I could see her making up characters to play with. Naturally she had to talk for her characters, or they would not say what she wanted them to. Most children play at that at times. I had done that extensively so I knew what she was doing when I saw her with the door half open, ringing her own doorbell and inviting herself to have some tea and muffins. When she was tired of her game, she just quit and was a grown woman again.

On another occasion, she called me up from the outside. She had been out for about two hours when she called me and told me to meet her at 67th Street and Columbus Avenue with her goloshes. She was not coming home immediately. She had to go somewhere else and she needed her goloshes. It was a gloomy day with snow and slush underfoot.

So, I grabbed up her goloshes and hurried down to the corner to wait for her to come along in a cab, as she had said. She warned me that she was at Columbus Circle and I would have to hurry, or she would be there before I was. I ran part of the way and was happy that I was there before her. I looked this a way and I looked that a way, but no Fanny Hurst peeping out of a cab. I waited from one foot to the other. The wind was searching me like the police. After a long wait I decided that something had detained her or changed her plans. Perhaps, she was trying to reach me on the phone. I hurried on back to Number 27 and went inside. Who was stretched out

194

on the divan, all draped in a gorgeous American Beauty rose housecoat, but Fanny Hurst! Been home such a long time that she was all draped and eating candy. It was not April, but she was playing April Fool on me. She never let on to me about that trick one way or another. She was grown again by then, and looking just as solemn as if she never played.

She likes for me to drive her, and we have made several tours. Her impishness broke out once on the road. She told me to have the car all serviced and ready for next morning. We were going up to Belgrade Lakes in Maine to pay Elizabeth Marbury a visit.

So soon next day we were on the road. She was Fanny Hurst, the famous author as far as Saratoga Springs. As we drove into the heart of town, she turned to me and said, "Zora, the water here at Saratoga is marvelous. Have you ever had any of it?"

"No, Miss Hurst, I never did."

"Then we must stop and let you have a drink. It would never do for you to miss having a drink of Saratoga water."

We parked near the famous United States Hotel and got out.

"It would be nice to stop over here for the night," she said. "I'll go see about the hotel. There is a fountain over there in the park. Be sure and get yourself a drink! You can take Lummox for a run while you get your water."

I took Lummox out of the car. To say I took Lummox for a run would be merely making a speech-figure. Lummox weighed about three pounds, and with his short legs, when he thought that he was running he was just jumping up and down in the same place. But anyway, I took him along to get the water. It was so-so as far as the taste went.

When I got back to the car, she was waiting for me. It was too early in the season for the hotel to be open. Too bad! She knew I would have enjoyed it so much. Well, I really ought to have some pleasure. Had I ever seen Niagara Falls?

"No, Miss Hurst. I always wanted to see it, but I never had a chance."

"Zora! You mean to tell me that you have never seen Niagara Falls?"

"No." I felt right sheepish about it when she put it that way.

"Oh, you must see the Falls. Get in the car and let's go. You must see those Falls right now." The way she sounded, my whole life was bare up to then and wrecked for the future unless I saw Niagara Falls.

The next afternoon around five o'clock, we were at Niagara Falls. It had been a lovely trip across Northern New York State.

"Here we are, now, Zora. Hurry up and take a good look at the Falls. I brought you all the way over here so that you could see them."

She didn't need to urge me. I leaned on the rail and looked and looked. It was worth the trip, all right. It was just like watching the Atlantic Ocean jump off of Pike's Peak.

In ten minutes or so, Miss Hurst touched me and I turned around.

"Zora, have you ever been across the International Bridge? I think you ought to see the Falls from the Canadian side. Come on, so you can see it from over there. It would be too bad for you to come all the way over here to see it and not see it from the Bridge."

So we drove across the Bridge. A Canadian Customs Official tackled us immediately. The car had to be registered. How long did we intend to stay?

"You'd better register it for two weeks," Miss Hurst answered and it was done. The sun was almost down.

"Look, Zora, Hamilton is only a short distance. I know you want to see it. Come on, let's drive on, and spend the night at Hamilton."

We drove on. I was surprised to see that everything in Canada looked so much like everything in the United States. It was deep twilight when we got into Hamilton.

"They tell me Kitchener is a most interesting little place, Zora. I know it would be fun to go on there and spend the night." So on to Kitchener we went.

Here was Fanny Hurst, a great artist and globe famous, behaving like a little girl, teasing her nurse to take her to the zoo, and having a fine time at it.

Well, we spent an exciting two weeks motoring over Ontario, seeing the country-side and eating at quaint but well-appointed inns. She was like a child at a circus. She was a run-away, with no responsibilities. A man in upper New York State dangled his old cherry trees at us as we drove homeward. He didn't have any business to do it. We parked and crept over into his old orchard and ate all we could, filled up our hats and drove on. Maybe he never missed them, but if he did, Miss Hurst said that it served him right for planting trees like that to dangle at people. Teach him a lesson. We came rolling south by east laughing, eating Royal Anne cherries and spitting seeds. It was glorious! Who has not eaten stolen fruit?

Fanny Hurst, the author, and the wife of Jacques Danielson, was not with us again until we hit Westchester on the way home. Then she replaced Mrs. Hurst's little Fanny and began to discuss her next book with me and got very serious in her manner.

While Fanny Hurst brings a very level head to her dressing, she exults in her new things like any debutante. She knows exactly what goes with her very white skin, black hair and sloe eyes, and she wears it. I doubt if any woman on earth has gotten better effects than she has with black, white and red. Not only that, she knows how to parade it when she gets it on. She will never be jailed for uglying up a town.

THIS ETHEL WATERS

I am due to have this friendship with Ethel Waters, because I worked for it.

She came to me across the footlights. Not the artist alone, but the person, and I wanted to know her very much. I was too timid to go backstage and haunt her, so I wrote her letters and she just plain ignored me. But I kept right on. I sensed

197

a great humanness and depth about her soul and I wanted to know someone like that.

Then Carl Van Vechten gave a dinner for me. A great many celebrities were there, including Sinclair Lewis, Dwight Fiske, Anna Mae Wong, Blanche Knopf, an Italian soprano, and my old friend, Jane Belo. Carl whispered to me that Ethel Waters was coming in later. He was fond of her himself and he knew I wanted to know her better, so he had persuaded her to come. Carl is given to doing nice things like that.

We got to talking, Ethel and I, and got on very well. Then I found that what I suspected, was true. Ethel Waters is a very shy person. It had not been her intention to ignore me. She had felt that I belonged to another world and had no need of her. She thought that I had been merely curious. She laughed at her error and said, "And here you were just like me all the time." She got warm and friendly, and we went on from there. When she was implored to sing, she asked me first what I wanted to hear. It was "Stormy Weather," of course, and she did it beautifully.

Then I did something for her. She told us that she was going to appear with Hall Johnson's Choir at Carnegie Hall, and planned to do some spirituals. Immediately, the Italian soprano and others present advised her not to do it. The argument was that Marian Anderson, Roland Hayes and Paul Robeson had sung them so successfully that her audience would make comparisons and Ethel would suffer by it. I saw the hurt in Ethel's face and jumped in. I objected that Ethel was not going to do any concertized versions of spirituals. She had never rubbed any hair off of her head against any college walls and she was not going to sing that way. She was going to sing those spirituals just the way her humble mother had sung them to her.

She turned to me with a warm, grateful smile on her face, and said, "Thank you."

When she got ready to leave, she got her wraps and said, "Come on, Zora. Let's go on uptown." I went along with her, her husband, and faithful Lashley, a young woman spiritual singer from somewhere in Mississippi, whom Ethel has taken under her wing.

We kept up with each other after that, and I got to know her very well. We exchanged confidences that really mean something to both of us. I am her friend, and her tongue is in my mouth. I can speak her sentiments for her, though Ethel Waters can do very well indeed in speaking for herself. She has a homely philosophy that reaches all corners of Life, and she has words to fit when she speaks.

She is one of the strangest bundles of people that I have ever met. You can just see the different folks wrapped up in her if you associate with her long. Just like watching an open fire—the color and shape of her personality is never the same twice. She has extraordinary talents which her lack of formal education prevents her from displaying. She never had a chance to go beyond the third grade in school. A terrible fear is in me that the world will never really know her. You have seen her and heard her on the stage, but so little of her capabilities gets seen. Her struggle for adequate expression throws her into moods at times. She said to me Christmas Day of 1941, "You have the advantage of me, Zora. I can only show what is on the stage. You can write a different kind of book each time."

She is a Catholic, and deeply religious. She plays a good game of bridge, but no card-playing at her house on Sundays. No more than her mother would have had in her house. Nobody is going to dance and cut capers around her on the Sabbath, either. What she sings about and acts out on the stage, has nothing to do with her private life.

Her background is most humble. She does not mind saying that she was born in the slums of Philadelphia in an atmosphere that smacked of the rural South. She neither drinks nor smokes and is always chasing me into a far corner of the room when I light a cigarette. She thanks God that I don't drink.

Her religious bent shows in unexpected ways. For instance, we were discussing her work in "Cabins in the Sky." She said, "When we started to rehearse the spirituals, some of those no-manners people started to swinging 'em, and get smart. I told 'em they better not play with God's music like that. I told 'em if I caught any of 'em at it, I'd knock 'em clean over into that orchestra pit." Her eyes flashed fire as she told me about it. Then she calmed down and laughed. "Of course, you know, Zora, God didn't want me to knock 'em over. That was an idea of mine."

And this fact of her background has a great deal to do with her approach to people. She is shy and you must convince her that she is really wanted before she will open up her tender parts and show you. Even in her career, I am persuaded that Ethel Waters does not know that she has arrived. For that reason, she is grateful for any show of love or appreciation. People to whom she has given her love and trust have exploited it heartlessly, like hogs under an acorn tree—guzzling and grabbing with their ears hanging over their eyes, and never looking up to see the high tree that the acorns fell off of.

She has been married twice, unhappily each time because I am certain that neither man could perceive her.

"I was thirteen when I married the first time," she confided to me. "And I was a virgin when I got married."

Now, she is in love with Archie Savage, who is a talented dancer, and formerly of the Dunham group. They met during the rehearsals for "Cabins in the Sky" and the affair is on! It looks as if they will make a wed, because they are eternally together. He has given her a taste for things outside the theater like art museums and the opera. He has sold her on the pictures, statues and paintings, but she says that this opera business sticks in her craw. She says she can't see why people fool with a thing like that that just isn't natural.

"Singing is music, Zora, but this Grand Opera is a game. The opera singers lay so much down that they can make that high note, and the audiences fades 'em the price of admission that they can't do it. Of course, all those high class folks that lay bets on high notes are good sports. If the singers haul off and win the bet, they give 'em a great big hand, and go outside for a smoke. And the only reason that opera houses don't make no more money than they do, is because so many more folks would rather bet on race horses. I don't bet on nothing because I don't think it's right. But if I did, my money would be on the horse."

Still if Sonny (our intimate name for Archie) wants to take her to the opera, she will go to please him. "He is fire and fuel to my life," she told me and played with her handkerchief like a teen-age girl.

She went on the stage at thirteen and says that she got eight dollars a week for her first salary. She was so frightened that she had to be pushed on to sing her song, and then another member of the cast had to come on with her until she could get started. Then too, they had to place a chair for her to lean on to overcome her nervousness.

At fifteen, she introduced the St. Louis Blues to the world. She saw a sheet of the music, had it played for her, then wrote to W. C. Handy for permission to use it. Handy answered on a postal card and told her to go as far as she liked, or words to that effect. If W. C. Handy had only known at that time the importance of his act!

She is gay and sombre by turns. I have listened to her telling a story and noticed her change of mood in mid-story. I have asked her to repeat something particularly pungent that she has said, and had her tell me, "I couldn't say it now. My thoughts are different. Sometime when I am thinking that same way, I'll tell it to you again."

The similes and metaphors just drip off of her lips. One day I sat in her living room on Hobart Street in Los Angeles, deep in thought. I had really forgotten that others were present. She nudged Archie Savage and pointed at me. "Salvation looking at the temple forlorn," she commented and laughed. "What you doing, Zora? Pasturing in your mind?"

"It's nice to be talking things over with you, Zora," she told me another time. "Conversation is the ceremony of companionship."

Speaking of a man we both know, she said, "The bigger lie he tells, the more guts he tells it with."

"That man's jaws are loaded with big words, but he never says a thing," she said speaking of a mutual friend. "He got his words out of a book. I got mine out of life."

"She shot him lightly and he died politely," she commented after reading in the *Los Angeles Examiner* about a woman killing her lover.

Commenting on a man who had used coarse language, she said, "I'd rather him to talk differently, but you can't hold him responsible, Zora, they are all the words he's got."

Ethel Waters has known great success and terrible personal tragedy, so she knows that no one can have everything.

"Don't care how good the music is, Zora, you can't dance on every set."

I am grateful for the friendship of Fanny Hurst and Ethel Waters. But how does one speak of honest gratitude? Who can know the outer ranges of friendship? I am tempted to say that no one can live without it. It seems to me that trying to live without friends, is like milking a bear to get cream for your morning coffee. It is a whole lot of trouble, and then not worth much after you get it.

CHAPTER 14

LOVE

What do I really know about love? I have had some experiences and feel fluent enough for my own satisfaction. Love, I find is like singing. Everybody can do enough to satisfy themselves, though it may not impress the neighbors as being very much. That is the way it is with me, but whether I know anything unusual, I couldn't say. Don't look for me to call a string of names and point out chapter and verse. Ladies do not kiss and tell any more than gentlemen do.

I have read many books where the heroine was in love for a long time without knowing it. I have talked with people and they have told me the same thing. So maybe that is the way it ought to be. That is not the way it is with me at all. I have been *out* of love with people for a long time, perhaps without finding it out. But when I fall *in,* I can feel the bump. That is a fact and I would not try to fool you. Love may be a sleepy, creeping thing with some others, but it is a mighty wakening thing with me. I feel the jar, and I know it from my head on down.

Though I started falling in love before I was seven years old, I never had a fellow until I was nearly grown. I was such a poor picker. I would have had better luck if I had stuck to boys around my own age, but that wouldn't do me. I wanted somebody with long pants on, and they acted as if they didn't know I was even born. The heartless wretches would walk right past my gate with grown women and pay me no attention at all, other than to say hello or something like that. Then I would have to look around for another future husband, only to have the same thing happen all over again.

Of course, in high school I received mushy notes and wrote them. A day or two, a week or month at most would see the end of the affair. Gone without a trace. I was in my freshman year in college when I first got excited, really.

He could stomp a piano out of this world, sing a fair baritone and dance beautifully. He noticed me, too, and I was carried away. For the first time since my mother's death, there was someone who felt really close and warm to me.

This affair went on all through my college life, with the exception of two fallings-out. We got married immediately after I finished my work at Barnard College, which should have been the happiest day of my life. St. Augustine, Florida, is a beautiful setting for such a thing.

But, it was not my happiest day. I was assailed by doubts. For the first time since I met him, I asked myself if I really were in love, or if this had been a habit. I had an uncomfortable feeling of unreality. The day and the occasion did not underscore any features of nature nor circumstance, and I wondered why. Who had cancelled the well-advertised tour of the moon? Somebody had turned a hose on the sun. What I had taken for eternity turned out to be a moment walking in its sleep.

After our last falling-out, he asked me please to forgive him, and I said that I did. But now, had I really? A wind full of memories blew out of the past and brought a chilling fog. This was not the expected bright dawn. Rather, some vagrant ray had played a trick on the night. I could not bring myself to tell him my thoughts. I just couldn't, no matter how hard I tried, but there they were crowding me from pillar to post.

Back in New York, I met Mrs. Mason and she offered me the chance to return to my research work, and I accepted it. It seemed a way out without saying anything very much. Let nature take its course. I did not tell him about the arrangement. Rather, I urged him to return to Chicago to continue his medical work. Then I stretched my shivering insides out and went back to work. I have seen him only once since then. He has married again, and I hope that he is happy.

Having made such a mess, I did not rush at any serious affair right away. I set to work and really worked in earnest. Work was to be all of me, so I said. Three years went by. I had finished that phase of research and was considering writing my first book, when I met the man who was really to lay me by the heels. I met P.M.P.

He was tall, dark brown, magnificently built, with a beautifully modelled back head. His profile was strong and good. The nose and lip were especially good front and side. But his looks only drew my eyes in the beginning. I did not fall in love with him just for that. He had a fine mind and that intrigued me. When a man keeps beating me to the draw mentally, he begins to get glamorous.

I did not just fall in love. I made a parachute jump. No matter which way I probed him, I found something more to admire. We fitted each other like a glove. His intellect got me first for I am the kind of a woman that likes to move on mentally from point to point, and I like for my man to be there way ahead of me. Then if he is strong and honest, it goes on from there. Good looks are not essential, just extra added attraction. He had all of those things and more. It seems to me that God must have put in extra time making him up. He stood on his own feet so firmly that he reared back.

To illustrate the point, I got into trouble with him for trying to loan him a quarter. It came about this way.

I lived in the Graham Court at 116th Street and Seventh Avenue. He lived down in 64th Street, Columbus Hill. He came to call one night and everything went off sweetly until he got ready to leave. At the door he told me to let him go because he was going to walk home. He had spent the only nickel he had that night to come to see me. That upset me, and I ran to get a quarter to loan him until his pay day. What did I do that for? He flew hot. In fact he was the hottest man in the five boroughs. Why did I insult him like that? The responsibility was all his. He had known that he did not have his return fare when he left home, but he had wanted to come, and so he had come. Let him take the consequences for his own acts. What kind of a coward did I take him for? How could he deserve my respect if he behaved like a cream puff? He was a *man*! No woman on earth could either lend him nor give him a cent. If a man could not do for a woman, what good was he on earth? His great desire was to do for me. *Please* let him be a *man*!

For a minute I was hurt and then I saw his point. He had done a beautiful thing and I was killing it off in my blindness. If it pleased him to walk all of that distance for my sake, it pleased him as evidence of his devotion. Then too, he wanted to do all the doing, and keep me on the receiving end. He soared in my respect from that moment on. Nor did he ever change. He meant to be the head, *so help him over the fence!*

That very manliness, sweet as it was, made us both suffer. My career balked the completeness of his ideal. I really wanted to conform, but it was impossible. To me there was no conflict. My work was one thing, and he was all of the rest. But, I could not make him see that. Nothing must be in my life but himself.

But, I am ahead of my story. I was interested in him for nearly two years before he knew it. A great deal happened between the time we met and the time we had any serious talk.

As I said, I loved, but I did not say so, because nobody asked me. I made up my mind to keep my feelings to myself since they did not seem to matter to anyone else but me.

I went South, did some more concert work and wrote *Jonah's Gourd Vine* and *Mules and Men,* then came back to New York.

He began to make shy overtures to me. I pretended not to notice for a while so that I could be sure and not be hurt. Then he gave me the extreme pleasure of telling me right out loud about it. It seems that he had been in love with me just as long as I had been with him, but he was afraid that I didn't mean him any good, as the saying goes. He had been trying to make me tell him something. He began by complimenting me on my clothes. Then one night when we had attended the Alpha Phi Alpha fraternity dance—yes, he is an Alpha man—he told me that the white dress I was wearing was beautiful, but I did not have on an evening wrap rich enough to suit him. He had in mind just the kind he wanted to see me in, and when he made the kind of money he expected to, the first thing he meant to do was to buy me a gorgeous evening wrap and everything to go with it. He wanted *his* wife to look swell. He looked at me from under his eyelashes to see how I was taking it. I smiled and so he went on.

"You know, Zora, you've got a real man on your hands. You've got somebody to do for you. I'm tired of seeing you work so hard. I wouldn't want *my* wife to do anything but look after me. Be home looking like Skookums when I got there."

He always said I reminded him of the Indian on the Skookum Apples, so I knew he meant me to understand that he wanted to be coming home to me, and with those words he endowed me with Radio City, the General Motors Corporation, the United States, Europe, Asia and some outlying continents. I had everything!

So actively began the real love affair of my life. He was then a graduate of City College, and was working for his Master's degree at Columbia. He had no money. He was born of West Indian parents in the Columbus Hill district of New York City, and had nothing to offer but what it takes—a bright soul, a fine mind in a fine body, and courage. He is so modest that I do not think that he yet knows his assets. That was to make trouble for us later on.

It was a curious situation. He was so extraordinary that I lived in terrible fear lest women camp on his doorstep in droves and take him away from me. I found out later on that he could not believe that I wanted just him. So there began an agonizing tug of war. Looking at a very serious photograph of me that Carl Van Vechten had made, he told me one night in a voice full of feeling that that was the way he wanted me to look all the time unless I was with him. I almost laughed out loud. That was just the way I felt. I hated to think of him smiling unless he was smiling at me. His grins were too precious to be wasted on ordinary mortals, especially women.

If he could only have realized what a lot he had to offer, he need not have suffered so much through doubting that he could hold me. I was hog-tied and branded, but he didn't realize it. He could make me fetch and carry, but he wouldn't believe it. So when I had to meet people on business, or went to literary parties and things like that, it would drive him into a sulk, and then he would make me unhappy. I too, failed to see how deeply he felt. I would interpret his moods as indifference and die, and die, and die.

He begged me to give up my career, marry him and live outside of New York City. I really wanted to do anything he wanted me to do, but that one thing I could not do. It was not just my contract with my publishers, it was that I had things clawing inside of me that must be said. I could not see that my work should make any difference in marriage. He was all and everything else to me but that. One did not conflict with the other in my mind. But it was different with him. He felt that he did not matter to me enough. He was the master kind. All, or nothing, for him.

The terrible thing was that we could neither leave each other alone, nor compromise. Let me seem too cordial with any male and something was going to happen. Just let him smile too broad at any woman, and no sooner did we get inside my door than the war was on! One night (I didn't decide this) something primitive inside me tore past the barriers and before I realized it, I had slapped his face. That was a mistake. He was still smoldering from an incident a week old. A fellow had met us on Seventh Avenue and kissed me on my cheek. Just one of those casual things, but it had burned up P.M.P. So I had unknowingly given him an opening he had been praying for. He paid me off then and there with interest. No broken bones, you understand, and no black eyes. I realized afterwards that my hot head could tell me to beat him, but it would cost me something. I would have to bring head to get head. I couldn't get his and leave mine locked up in the dresser-drawer.

Then I knew I was too deeply in love to be my old self. For always a blow to my body had infuriated me beyond measure. Even with my parents, that was true. But somehow, I didn't hate him at all. We sat down on the floor and each one of us tried to take all the blame. He went out and bought some pie and I made a pot of hot chocolate and we were more affectionate than ever. The next day he made me a book case that I needed and you couldn't get a pin between us.

But fate was watching us and laughing. About a month later when he was with me, the telephone rang. Would I please come down to an apartment in the Fifties and meet an out-of-town celebrity? He was in town for only two days and he wanted to meet me before he left. When I turned from the phone, P.M.P. was changed. He begged me not to go. I reminded him that I had promised, and begged him to come along. He refused and walked out. I went, but I was most unhappy.

This sort of thing kept up time after time. He would not be reconciled to the thing. We were alternately the happiest people in the world, and the most miserable. I suddenly decided to go away to see if I could live without him. I did not even tell him that I was going. But I wired him from some town in Virginia.

Miss Barnicle of New York University asked me to join her and Alan Lomax on a short bit of research. I was to select the area and contact the subjects. Alan Lomax was joining us with a recording machine. So because I was delirious with joy and pain, I suddenly decided to leave New York and see if I could come to some decision. I knew no more at the end than I did when I went South. Six weeks later I was back in New York and just as much his slave as ever.

Really, I never had occasion to doubt his sincerity, but I used to drag my heart over hot coals by supposing. I did not know that I could suffer so. Then all of my careless words came to haunt me. For theatrical effect, I had uttered sacred words and oaths to others before him. How I hated myself for the sacrilege now! It would have seemed so wonderful never to have uttered them before.

But no matter how soaked we were in ecstasy, the telephone or the door bell would ring, and there would be my career again. A charge had been laid upon me and I must follow the call. He said once with pathos in his voice, that at times he could not feel my presence. My real self had escaped him. I could tell from both his face and his voice that it hurt him terribly. It hurt me just as much to see him hurt. He really had nothing to worry about, but I could not make him see it. So there we were. Caught in a fiendish trap. We could not leave each other alone, and we could not shield each other from hurt. Our bitterest enemies could not have contrived more exquisite torture for us.

Another phase troubled me. As soon as he took his second degree, he was in line for bigger and better jobs. I began to feel that our love was slowing down his efforts. He had brains and character. He ought to go a long way. I grew terribly afraid that later on he would feel that I had thwarted him in a way and come to resent me. That was a scorching thought. Even if I married him, what about five years from now, the way we were going?

In the midst of this, I received my Guggenheim fellowship. This was my chance to release him, and fight myself free from my obsession. He would get over me in a few months and go on to be a very big man. So I sailed off to Jamaica. But I freely admit that everywhere I set my feet down, there were tracks of blood. Blood from the very middle of my heart. I did not write because if I had written and he answered my letter, everything would have broken down.

So I pitched in to work hard on my research to smother my feelings. But the thing would not down. The plot was far from the circumstances, but I tried to embalm all the tenderness of my passion for him in *Their Eyes Were Watching God.*

When I returned to America after nearly two years in the Caribbean, I found that he had left his telephone number with my publishers. For some time, I did not use it. Not because I did not want to, but because the moment when I should hear his voice something would be in wait for me. It might be warm and eager. It might be cool and impersonal, just with overtones from the grave of things. So I went south and stayed several months before I ventured to use it. Even when I returned to New York it took me nearly two months to get up my courage. When I did make the call, I cursed myself for the delay. Here was the shy, warm man I had left.

Then we met and talked. We both were stunned by the revelation that all along we had both thought and acted desperately in exile, and all to no purpose. We were still in the toils and after all my agony, I found out that he was a sucker for me, and he found out that I was in his bag. And I had a triumph that only a woman could understand. He had not turned into a tramp in my absence, but neither had he flamed like a newborn star in his profession. He confessed that he needed my aggravating presence to push him. He had settled down to a plodding desk job and reconciled himself. He had let his waistline go a bit and that bespoke his inside feeling. That made me happy no end. No woman wants a man all finished and perfect. You have to have something to work on and prod. That waistline went down in a jiffy and he began to discuss work-plans with enthusiasm. He could see something ahead of him besides time. I was happy. If he had been crippled in both legs, it would have suited me even better.

What will be the end? That is not for me to know. Life poses questions and that two-headed spirit that rules the beginning and end of things called Death, has all the answers. And even if I did know all, I am supposed to have some private business to myself. What I do know, I have no intention of putting but so much in the public ears.

Perhaps the oath of Hercules shall always defeat me in love.

Once when I was small and first coming upon the story of "The Choice of Hercules," I was so impressed that I swore an oath to leave all pleasure and take the hard road of labor. Perhaps God heard me and wrote down my words in His book. I have thought so at times. Be that as it may, I have the satisfaction of knowing that I have loved and been loved by the perfect man. If I never hear of love again, I have known the real thing.

So much for what I know about the major courses in love. However, there are some minor courses which I have not grasped so well, and would be thankful for some coaching and advice.

First is the number of men who pant in my ear on short acquaintance, "You passionate thing! I can see you are just *burning* up! Most men would be disappointing to you. It takes a man like me for you. Ahhh! I know that you will just wreck me! Your eyes and your lips tell me a lot. You are a walking furnace!" This amazes me sometimes. Often when this is whispered gustily into my ear, I am feeling no more amorous than a charter member of the Union League Club. I may be thinking of turnip greens with dumplings, or more royalty checks, and here is a man who visualizes me on a divan sending the world up in smoke. It has happened so often that I have come to expect it. There must be something about me that looks sort of couchy. Maybe it is a birth-mark. My mother could have been frightened by a bed. There is nothing to be done about it, I suppose. But, I must say about these mirages that seem to rise around me, that the timing is way off on occasion.

Number two is, a man may lose interest in me and go where his fancy leads him, and we can still meet as friends. But if I get tired and let on about it, he is certain to become an enemy of mine. That forces me to lie like the cross-ties from New York to Key West. I have learned to frame it so that I can claim to be deserted and devastated by him. Then he goes off with a sort of twilight tenderness for me, wondering what it is that he's got that brings so many women down! I do not even have to show real tears. All I need to do is show my stricken face and dash away from him to hide my supposed heartbreak and renunciation. He understands that I am fleeing before his allure so that I can be firm in my resolution to save the pieces. He knew all along that he was a hard man to resist, so he visualized my dampened pillow. It is a good thing that some of them have sent roses as a poultice and stayed away. Otherwise, they might have found the poor, heartbroken wreck of a thing all dressed to kill and gone out for a high-heel time with the new interest, who has the new interesting things to say and do. Now, how to break off without acting deceitful and still keep a friend?

Number three is kin to Number two, in a way. Under the spell of moonlight, music, flowers or the cut and smell of good tweeds, I sometimes feel the divine urge for an hour, a day or maybe a week. Then it is gone and my interest returns to corn pone and mustard greens, or rubbing a paragraph with a soft cloth. Then my ex-sharer of a mood calls up in a fevered voice and reminds me of every silly thing I said, and eggs me on to say them all over again. It is the third presentation of turkey hash after Christmas. It is asking me to be a seven-sided liar. Accuses me of being faithless and inconsistent if I don't. There is no inconsistency there. I was sincere for the moment in which I said the things. It is strictly a matter of time. It was true for the moment, but the next day or the next week, is not that moment. No two moments are any more alike than two snowflakes. Like snowflakes, they get that same look from being so plentiful and falling so close together. But examine them closely and see the multiple differences between them. Each moment has its own task and capacity, and doesn't melt down like snow and form again. It keeps its character forever. So the great difficulty lies in trying to transpose last night's moment to a day which has no knowledge of it. That look, that tender touch, was issued by the mint of the richest of all kingdoms. That same expression of today is utter counterfeit, or at best the wildest of inflation. What could be more zestless than passing out cancelled checks? It is wrong to be called faithless under circumstances like that. What to do?

I have a strong suspicion, but I can't be sure that much that passes for constant love is a golded-up moment walking in its sleep. Some people know that it is the walk of the dead, but in desperation and desolation, they have staked everything on life after death and the resurrection, so they haunt the grave-yard. They build an altar on the tomb and wait there like faithful Mary for the stone to roll away. So the moment has authority over all of their lives. They pray constantly for the miracle of the moment to burst its bonds and spread out over time.

But pay no attention to what I say about love, for as I said before, it may not mean a thing. It is my own bath-tub singing. Just because my mouth opens up like a prayer book, it does not just have to flap like a Bible. And then again, anybody whose mouth is cut cross-ways is given to lying, unconsciously as well as knowingly. So pay my few scattering remarks no mind as to love in general. I only know my part.

Anyway, it seems to be the unknown country from which no traveler ever returns. What seems to be a returning pilgrim is another person born in the strange country with the same-looking ears and hands. He is a stranger to the person who fared forth, and a stranger to family and old friends. He is clothed in mystery henceforth and forever. So, perhaps no-body knows, or can tell, any more than I. Maybe the old Negro folk-rhyme tells all there is to know:

> Love is a funny thing; Love is a blossom;
> If you want your finger bit, poke it at a possum.

CHAPTER 15

RELIGION

You wouldn't think that a person who was born with God in the house would ever have any questions to ask on the subject.

But as early as I can remember, I was questing and seeking. It was not that I did not hear. I tumbled right into the Missionary Baptist Church when I was born. I saw the preachers and the pulpits, the people and the pews. Both at home and from the pulpit, I heard my father, known to thousands as "Reverend Jno" (an abbreviation for John) explain all about God's habits, His heaven, His ways, and Means. Everything was known and settled.

From the pews I heard a ready acceptance of all that Papa said. Feet beneath the pews beat out a rhythm as he pictured the scenery of heaven. Heads nodded with conviction in time to Papa's words. Tense snatches of tune broke out and some shouted until they fell into a trance at the recognition of what they heard from the pulpit. Come "love feast"* some of the

---

*The "Love Feast" or "Experience Meeting" is a meeting held either the Friday night or the Sunday morning before Communion. Since no one is supposed to take Communion unless he or she is in harmony with all other members, there are great

congregation told of getting close enough to peep into God's sitting room windows. Some went further. They had been inside the place and looked all around. They spoke of sights and scenes around God's throne.

That should have been enough for me. But somehow it left a lack in my mind. They should have looked and acted differently from other people after experiences like that. But these people looked and acted like everybody else—or so it seemed to me. They ploughed, chopped wood, went possum-hunting, washed clothes, raked up back-yards and cooked collard greens like anybody else. No more ornaments and nothing. It mystified me. There were so many things they neglected to look after while they were right there in the presence of All-Power. I made up my mind to do better than that if ever I made the trip.

I wanted to know, for instance, why didn't God make grown babies instead of those little measly things that messed up didies and cried all the time? What was the sense in making babies with no teeth? He knew that they had to have teeth, didn't He? So why not give babies their teeth in the beginning instead of hiding the toothless things in hollow stumps and logs for grannies and doctors to find and give to people? He could see all the trouble people had with babies, rubbing their gums and putting wood-lice around their necks to get them to cut teeth. Why did God hate for children to play on Sundays? If Christ, God's son, hated to die, and God hated for Him to die and have everybody grieving over it ever since, why did He have to do it? Why did people die anyway?

It was explained to me that Christ died to save the world from sin and then too, so that folks did not have to die anymore. That was a simple, clear-cut explanation. But then I heard my father and other preachers accusing people of sin. They went so far as to say that people were so prone to sin, that they sinned with every breath they drew. You couldn't

_____

protestations of love and friendship. It is an opportunity to re-affirm faith plus anything the imagination might dictate.

even breathe without sinning! How could that happen if we had already been saved from it? So far as the dying part was concerned, I saw enough funerals to know that somebody was dying. It seemed to me that somebody had been fooled and I so stated to my father and two of his colleagues. When they got through with me, I knew better than to say that out loud again, but their shocked and angry tirades did nothing for my bewilderment. My head was full of misty fumes of doubt.

Neither could I understand the passionate declarations of love for a being that nobody could see. Your family, your puppy and the new bull-calf, yes. But a spirit away off who found fault with everybody all the time, that was more than I could fathom. When I was asked if I loved God, I always said yes because I knew that that was the thing I was supposed to say. It was a guilty secret with me for a long time. I did not dare ask even my chums if they meant it when they said they loved God with all their souls and minds and hearts, and would be glad to die if He wanted them to. Maybe they had found out how to do it, and I was afraid of what they might say if they found out I hadn't. Maybe they wouldn't even play with me anymore.

As I grew, the questions went to sleep in me. I just said the words, made the motions and went on. My father being a preacher, and my mother superintendent of the Sunday School, I naturally was always having to do with religious ceremonies. I even enjoyed participation at times; I was moved, not by the spirit, but by action, more or less dramatic.

I liked revival meetings particularly. During these meetings the preacher let himself go. God was called by all of His praise-giving names. The scenery of heaven was described in detail. Hallelujah Avenue and Amen Street were paved with gold so fine that you couldn't drop a pea on them but what they rang like chimes. Hallelujah Avenue ran north and south across heaven, and was tuned to sound alto and bass. Amen Street ran east and west and was tuned to "treble" and tenor. These streets crossed each other right in front of the throne and made harmony all the time. Yes, and right there on that

217

corner was where all the loved ones who had gone on before would be waiting for those left behind.

Oh yes! They were all there in their white robes with the glittering crowns on their heads, golden girdles clasped about their waists and shoes of jewelled gold on their feet, singing the hallelujah song and waiting. And as they walked up and down the golden streets, their shoes would sing, "sol me, sol do" at every step.

Hell was described in dramatic fury. Flames of fire leaped up a thousand miles from the furnaces of Hell, and raised blisters on a sinning man's back before he hardly got started downward. Hell-hounds pursued their ever-dying souls. Everybody under the sound of the preacher's voice was warned, while yet they were on pleading terms with mercy, to take steps to be sure that they would not be a brand in that eternal burning.

Sinners lined the mourner's bench from the opening night of the revival. Before the week was over, several or all of them would be "under conviction." People, solemn of face, crept off to the woods to "praying ground" to seek religion. Every church member worked on them hard, and there was great clamor and rejoicing when any of them "come through" religion.

The pressure on the unconverted was stepped up by music and high drama. For instance I have seen my father stop preaching suddenly and walk down to the front edge of the pulpit and breathe into a whispered song. One of his most effective ones was:

> Run! Run! Run to the City of Refuge, children!
> Run! Oh, run! Or else you'll be consumed.

The congregation working like a Greek chorus behind him, would take up the song and the mood and hold it over for a while even after he had gone back into the sermon at high altitude:

Are you ready-ee? Hah!
For that great day, hah!
When the moon shall drape her face in mourning, hah!
And the sun drip down in blood, hah!
When the stars, hah!
Shall burst forth from their diamond sockets, hah!
And the mountains shall skip like lambs, hah!
Havoc will be there, my friends, hah!
With her jaws wide open, hah!
And the sinner-man, hah!
He will run to the rocks, hah!
And cry, Oh rocks! Hah!
Hide me! Hah!
Hide me from the face of an angry God, hah!
Hide me, Ohhhhhh!
But the rocks shall cry, hah!
Git away! Sinner man git away, hah!

(Tense harmonic chant seeps over the audience.)

You run to de rocks,
CHORUS: You can't hide
SOLOIST: Oh, you run to de rocks
CHORUS: Can't hide
SOLOIST: Oh, run to de mountain, you can't hide
ALL: Can't hide sinner, you can't hide.
Rocks cry, I'm burning too, hah!
In the eternal burning, hah!
Sinner man! Hah!
Where will you stand? Hah!
In that great gittin'-up morning? Hah!

The congregation would be right in there at the right moment bearing Papa up and heightening the effect of the fear-
some picture a hundred-fold. The more susceptible would be
swept away on the tide and "come through" shouting, and the
most reluctant would begin to waver. Seldom would there be
anybody left at the mourners' bench when the revival meeting
was over. I have seen my father "bring through" as many as

219

seventy-five in one two-week period of revival. Then a day would be set to begin the induction into the regular congregation. The first thing was to hear their testimony or Christian experience, and thus the congregation could judge whether they had really "got religion" or whether they were faking and needed to be sent back to "lick de calf over" again.

It was exciting to hear them tell their "visions." This was known as admitting people to the church on "Christian experience." This was an exciting time.

These visions are traditional. I knew them by heart as did the rest of the congregation, but still it was exciting to see how the converts would handle them. Some of them made up new details. Some of them would forget a part and improvise clumsily or fill up the gap with shouting. The audience knew, but everybody acted as if every word of it was new.

First they told of suddenly becoming conscious that they had to die. They became conscious of their sins. They were Godly sorry. But somehow, they could not believe. They started to pray. They prayed and they prayed to have their sins forgiven and their souls converted. While they laid under conviction, the hell-hounds pursued them as they ran for salvation. They hung over Hell by one strand of hair. Outside of the meeting, any of the listeners would have laughed at the idea of anybody with hair as close to their heads as ninety-nine is to a hundred hanging over Hell or anywhere else by a strand of that hair. But it was part of the vision and the congregation shuddered and groaned at the picture in a fervent manner. The vision must go on. While the seeker hung there, flames of fire leaped up and all but destroyed their ever-dying souls. But they called on the name of Jesus and immediately that dilemma was over. They then found themselves walking over Hell on a foot-log so narrow that they had to put one foot right in front of the other while the howling hell-hounds pursued them relentlessly. Lord! They saw no way of rescue. But they looked on the other side and saw a little white man and he called to them to come there. So they called the name of Jesus and suddenly they were on the other side. He poured the oil

220

of salvation into their souls and, hallelujah! They never expect to turn back. But still they wouldn't believe. So they asked God, if he had saved their souls, to give them a sign. If their sins were forgiven and their souls set free, please move that big star in the west over to the east. The star moved over. But still they wouldn't believe. If they were really saved, please move that big oak tree across the road. The tree skipped across the road and kept on growing just like it had always been there. Still they didn't believe. So they asked God for one more sign. Would He please make the sun shout so they could be sure. At that God got mad and said He had shown them all the signs He intended to. If they still didn't believe, He would send their bodies to the grave, where the worm never dies, and their souls to Hell, where the fire is never quenched. So then they cried out "I believe! I believe!" Then the dungeon shook and their chains fell off. "Glory! I know I got religion! I know I been converted and my soul set free! I never will forget that day when the morning star bust in my soul. I never expect to turn back!"

The convert shouted. Ecstatic cries, snatches of chants, old converts shouting in frenzy with the new. When the tumult finally died down, the pastor asks if the candidate is acceptable and there is unanimous consent. He or she is given the right hand of fellowship, and the next candidate takes the floor. And so on to the end.

I know now that I liked that part because it was high drama. I liked the baptisms in the lake too, and the funerals for the same reason. But of the inner thing, I was right where I was when I first began to seek answers.

Away from the church after the emotional fire had died down, there were little jokes about some of the testimony. For instance a deacon said in my hearing, "Sister Seeny ought to know better than to be worrying God about moving the sun for her. She asked Him to move de tree to convince her, and He done it. Then she took and asked Him to move a star for her and He done it. But when she kept on worrying Him about moving the sun, He took and told her, says, 'I don't mind moving that tree for you, and I don't mind moving a star just to pacify your mind, because I got plenty of *them.* I ain't got but one sun, Seeny, and I ain't going to be shoving it around to please you and nobody else. I'd like mighty much for you to believe, but if you can't believe without me moving my sun for you, you can just go right on to Hell.' "

The thing slept on in me until my college years without any real decision. I made the necessary motions and forgot to think. But when I studied both history and philosophy, the struggle began again.

When I studied the history of the great religions of the world, I saw that even in his religion, man carried himself along. His worship of strength was there. God was made to look that way too. We see the Emperor Constantine, as pagan as he could lay in his hide, having his famous vision of the cross with the injunction: *"In Hoc Signo Vinces,"* and arising next day not only to win a great battle, but to start out on his missionary journey with his sword. He could not sing like Peter, and he could not preach like Paul. He probably did not even have a good straining voice like my father to win converts and influence people. But he had his good points—one of them being a sword—and a seasoned army. And the way he brought sinners to repentance was nothing short of miraculous. Whole tribes and nations fell under conviction just as soon as they heard he was on the way. They did not wait for any stars to move, nor trees to jump the road. By the time he crossed the border, they knew they had been converted. Their testimony was in on Christian experience and they were all ready for the right hand of fellowship and baptism. It seems that Reverend Brother Emperor Constantine carried the gospel up and down Europe with his revival meetings to such an extent that Christianity really took on. In Rome where Christians had been looked upon as rather indifferent lion-bait at best, and as keepers of virgins in their homes for no real good to the virgins among other things at their worst, Christianity mounted. Where before, Emperors could scarcely find enough of them to keep the spectacles going, now they were everywhere, in places high and low. The arrow had left the bow. Christianity was on its way to world power that would last. That was only the beginning. Military power was to be called in time and time again to carry forward the gospel of peace. There is not apt to be any difference of opinion between you and a dead man.

It was obvious that two men, both outsiders, had given my religion its chances of success. First the apostle Paul, who had been Saul, the erudite Pharisee, had arisen with a vision when he fell off of his horse on the way to Damascus. He not only formulated the religion, but exerted his brilliant mind to carry it to the most civilized nations of his time. Then Constantine took up with force where Paul left off with persuasion.

I saw the same thing with different details, happen in all the other great religions, and seeing these things, I went to thinking and questing again. I have achieved a certain peace within myself, but perhaps the seeking after the inner heart of truth will never cease in me. All sorts of interesting speculations arise.

Will military might determine the dominant religion of tomorrow? Who knows? Maybe Franklin Delano Roosevelt will fall on his head tomorrow and arise with a vision of Father Divine in the sky and the motto, "Peace! It's wonderful!" glowing like a rainbow above it.

Maybe our President would not even have to fall off of a horse, or a battleship, as the case might be. If Father Divine should come to control thirty million votes, the President could just skip the fall; that is, off of the horse.

Then, we might hear the former Franklin D. Roosevelt addressed as Sincere Determination. Eleanor would be Divine Eternal Commutation. Celestial Bountiful Tribulations would be Sister Frances Perkins. Harry Hopkins, Angelic Saintly Shadow. His Vocal Honor, La Guardia, would be known as Always Sounding Trumpet, and on his evident good works in his nursery, Harold Ickes would be bound to win the title of Fruitful Love Abounding.

Things getting into a fix like that, Sincere Determination,

being Arch Angel in the first degree, could have the honor of handing Father Divine his first bite at every meal. Celestial B. Tribulations would be in the kitchen dividing the opinion of the cooks. Eleanor, Divine Commutation, would be a Tidings-Angel, spreading the new gospel far and wide.

The Senate Chamber would be something to see. All of the seats in the center taken out and a long table loaded down with baked hams, turkeys, cakes and pies all ready for the legislative session to begin. With Father Divine at the head and Sincere Determination at the foot, slicing ham and turkey for the saints, there might not be much peace, but the laws would be truly wonderful. The saints would not overeat, either; what with being forced to raise their hands and cry "Peace!" every time Father Divine spoke and "it's truly wonderful" every time Sincere Determination uttered a sound, their eating would be negligible.

It would be a most holy conclave around that table. Sincere Determination would naturally be Senate president, seated under a huge picture of Father Divine. There would be no more disturbing debates and wrangling. The Lord would pass the law to Sincere Determination and he would pass it on to the Senate. The Senate would pass their plates for more ham and salad.

Father Divine would confine himself to pontifical audiences and meditation. He might even get himself a shoe embroidered with a quart or two of jewels for the dowagers of Park Avenue, Beacon Street and Sutton Place to have the extreme pleasure of kissing. His foot would be in it, of course. He wouldn't belittle a lady by sending out a cold shoe for impressively devout lady-angels to kiss like that.

Naturally, Sincere Determination would be able to read the Divine mind and then pass on which ones rated crowns of empire and which didn't. It would be the privilege of our Angelic Admirals and generals, "Puissant Defenders of the Faith," to demote all infidels and correct all typographical errors, emperor to impotent, and vice versa; according as a man worships, so is he, as the saying goes.

Naturally, there would be no more private money. Father would hold it all for everybody. No more just homes. Every house a "heaven." Peace!

Our holy fighting men would have high arching wings that covered up their mouths but left their ears wide open—a splendid type of fighting saints.

Don't think this impossible because of certain natural difficulties. Father Divine's looks need not be any drawback, nor a stumbling stone to our religious faith. Just let him collect enough votes and he will be a sure-enough pretty man in this world. Men with no more personal looks than he have founded all of our great religions. After all, the cradle of a creed is no Hollywood casting office.

So, having looked at the subject from many sides, studied beliefs by word of mouth and then as they fit into great rigid forms, I find I know a great deal about form, but little or nothing about the mysteries I sought as a child. As the ancient tent-maker said, I have come out of the same door wherein I went.

But certain things have seemed to me to be true as I heard the tongues of those who had speech, and listened at the lips of books. It seems to me to be true that heavens are placed in the sky because it is the unreachable. The unreachable and therefore the unknowable always seem divine—hence, religion. People need religion because the great masses fear life and its consequences. Its responsibilities weigh heavy. Feeling a weakness in the face of great forces, men seek an alliance with omnipotence to bolster up their feeling of weakness, even though the omnipotence they rely upon is a creature of their own minds. It gives them a feeling of security. Strong, self-determining men are notorious for their lack of reverence. Constantine, having converted millions to Christianity by the sword, himself refused the consolation of Christ until his last hour. Some say not even then.

As for me, I do not pretend to read God's mind. If He has a plan of the Universe worked out to the smallest detail, it would be folly for me to presume to get down on my knees and attempt to revise it. That, to me, seems the highest form of sacrilege. So I do not pray. I accept the means at my disposal for working out my destiny. It seems to me that I have been given a mind and will-power for that very purpose. I do not expect God to single me out and grant me advantages over my fellow men. Prayer is for those who need it. Prayer seems to me a cry of weakness, and an attempt to avoid, by trickery, the rules of the game as laid down. I do not choose to admit weakness. I accept the challenge of responsibility. Life, as it is, does not frighten me, since I have made my peace with the universe as I find it, and bow to its laws. The ever-sleepless sea in its bed, crying out "how long?" to Time; million-formed and never motionless flame; the contemplation of these two aspects alone, affords me sufficient food for ten spans of my expected lifetime. It seems to me that organized creeds are collections of words around a wish. I feel no need for such. However, I would not, by word or deed, attempt to deprive another of the consolation it affords. It is simply not for me. Somebody else may have my rapturous glance at the archangels. The springing of the yellow line of morning out of the misty deep of dawn, is glory enough for me. I know that nothing is destructible; things merely change forms. When the consciousness we know as life ceases, I know that I shall still be part and parcel of the world. I was a part before the sun rolled into shape and burst forth in the glory of change. I was, when the earth was hurled out from its fiery rim. I shall return with the earth to Father Sun, and still exist in substance when the sun has lost its fire, and disintegrated in infinity to perhaps become a part of the whirling rubble in space. Why fear? The stuff of my being is matter, ever changing, ever moving, but never lost; so what need of denominations and creeds to deny myself the comfort of all my fellow men? The wide belt of the universe has no need for finger-rings. I am one with the infinite and need no other assurance.

CHAPTER 16

LOOKING THINGS OVER

Well, that is the way things stand up to now. I can look back and see sharp shadows, high lights, and smudgy inbetweens. I have been in Sorrow's kitchen and licked out all the pots. Then I have stood on the peaky mountain wrappen in rainbows, with a harp and a sword in my hands.

What I had to swallow in the kitchen has not made me less glad to have lived, nor made me want to low-rate the human race, nor any whole sections of it. I take no refuge from myself in bitterness. To me, bitterness is the under-arm odor of wishful weakness. It is the graceless acknowledgment of defeat. I have no urge to make any concessions like that to the world as yet. I might be like that some day, but I doubt it. I am in the struggle with the sword in my hands, and I don't intend to run until you run me. So why give off the smell of something dead under the house while I am still in there tussling with my sword in my hand?

If tough breaks have not soured me, neither have my glory-moments caused me to build any altars to myself where I can burn incense before God's best job of work. My sense of humor will always stand in the way of my seeing myself, my family, my race or my nation as the whole intent of the universe. When I see what we really are like, I know that God is too great an artist for we folks on my side of the creek to be all of His best works. Some of His finest touches are among us, without doubt, but some more of His masterpieces are among those folks who live over the creek.

I see too, that while we all talk about justice more than any other quality on earth, there is no such thing as justice in the absolute in the world. We are too human to conceive of it. We all want the breaks, and what seems just to us is something that favors our wishes. If we did not feel that way, there would be no monuments to conquerors in our high places. It is obvious that the successful warrior is great to us because he went and took things from somebody else that we could use, and made the vanquished pay dearly for keeping it from us so long. To us, our man-of-arms is almost divine in that he seized good things from folks who could not appreciate them (well, not like we could, anyway) and brought them where they belonged. Nobody wants to hear anything about the side of the conquered. Any remarks from him is rebellion. This attitude does not arise out of studied cruelty, but out of the human bent that makes us feel that the man who wants the same thing we want, must be a crook and needs a good killing. "Look at the miserable creature!" we shout in justification. "Too weak to hold what we want!"

So looking back and forth in history and around the temporary scene, I do not visualize the moon dripping down in blood, nor the sun batting his fiery eyes and laying down in the cradle of eternity to rock himself into sleep and slumber at instances of human self-bias. I know that the sun and the moon must be used to sights like that by now. I too yearn for universal justice, but how to bring it about is another thing. It is such a complicated thing, for justice, like beauty is in the eye of the beholder. There is universal agreement of the principle, but the application brings on the fight. Oh, for some disinterested party to pass on things! Somebody will hurry to tell me that we voted God to the bench for that. But the lawyers who interpret His opinions, make His decisions sound just like they made them up themselves. Being an idealist, I too wish that the world was better than I am. Like all the rest of my fellow men, I don't want to live around people with no more principles than I have. My inner fineness is continually outraged at finding that the world is a whole family of Hurstons.

Seeing these things, I have come to the point by trying to make the day at hand a positive thing, and realizing the uselessness of gloominess.

Therefore, I see nothing but futility in looking back over my shoulder in rebuke at the grave of some white man who has been dead too long to talk about. That is just what I would be doing in trying to fix the blame for the dark days of slavery and the Reconstruction. From what I can learn, it was sad. Certainly. But my ancestors who lived and died in it are dead. The white men who profited by their labor and lives are dead also. I have no personal memory of those times, nor no responsibility for them. Neither has the grandson of the man who held my folks. So I see no need in button-holing that grandson like the Ancient Mariner did the wedding guest and calling for the High Sheriff to put him under arrest.

I am not so stupid as to think that I would be bringing this descendant of a slave-owner any news. He has heard just as much about the thing as I have. I am not so humorless as to visualize this grandson falling out on the sidewalk before me, and throwing an acre of fits in remorse because his old folks held slaves. No, indeed! If it happened to be a fine day and he had had a nice breakfast, he might stop and answer me like this:

"In the first place, I was not able to get any better view of social conditions from my grandmother's womb than you could from your grandmother's. Let us say for the sake of argument that I detest the institution of slavery and all that it implied, just as much as you do. You must admit that I was no more powerful to do anything about it in my unborn state than you were in yours. Why fix your eyes on me? I respectfully refer you to my ancestors, and bid you a good day."

If I still lingered before him, he might answer me further by asking questions like this:

"Are you so simple as to assume that the Big Surrender (Note: The South, both black and white speak of Lee's surrender to Grant as the Big Surrender) banished the concept of human slavery from the earth? What is the principle of slavery? Only the literal buying and selling of human flesh on the block? That was only an outside symbol. Real slavery is couched in the desire and the efforts of any man or community to live and advance their interests at the expense of the lives and interests of others. All of the outward signs come out of that. Do you not realize that the power, prestige and prosperity of the greatest nations on earth rests on colonies and sources of raw materials? Why else are great wars waged? If you have not thought, then why waste up time with your vapid accusations? If you have, then why single *me* out?" And like Pilate, he will light a cigar, and stroll on off without waiting for an answer.

Anticipating such an answer, I have no intention of wasting my time beating on old graves with a club. I know that I cannot pry aloose the clutching hand of Time, so I will turn all my thoughts and energies on the present. I will settle for from now on.

And why not? For me to pretend that I am Old Black Joe and waste my time on his problems, would be just as ridiculous as for the government of Winston Churchill to bill the Duke of Normandy the first of every month, or for the Jews to hang around the pyramids trying to picket Old Pharaoh. While I have a handkerchief over my eyes crying over the landing of the first slaves in 1619, I might miss something swell that is going on in 1942. Furthermore, if somebody were to consider my grandmother's ungranted wishes, and give *me* what *she* wanted, I would be too put out for words.

What do I want, then? I will tell you in a parable. A Negro deacon was down on his knees praying at a wake held for a

sister who had died that day. He had his eyes closed and was going great guns, when he noticed that he was not getting anymore "amens" from the rest. He opened his eyes and saw that everybody else was gone except himself and the dead woman. Then he saw the reason. The supposedly dead woman was trying to sit up. He bolted for the door himself, but it slammed shut so quickly that it caught his flying coat-tails and held him sort of static. "Oh, no, Gabriel!" the deacon shouted, "dat ain't no way for you to do. I can do my own running, but you got to 'low me the same chance as the rest."

I don't know any more about the future than you do. I hope that it will be full of work, because I have come to know by experience that work is the nearest thing to happiness that I can find. No matter what else I have among the things that humans want, I go to pieces in a short while if I do not work. What all my work shall be, I don't know that either, every hour being a stranger to you until you live it. I want a busy life, a just mind and a timely death.

But if I should live to be very old, I have laid plans for that so that it will not be too tiresome. So far, I have never used coffee, liquor, nor any form of stimulant. When I get old, and my joints and bones tell me about it, I can sit around and write for myself, if for nobody else, and read slowly and carefully the mysticism of the East, and re-read Spinoza with love and care. All the while my days can be a succession of coffee cups. Then when the sleeplessness of old age attacks me, I can have a likker bottle snug in my pantry and sip away and sleep. Get mellow and think kindly of the world. I think I can be like that because I have known the joy and pain of deep friendship. I have served and been served. I have made some good enemies for which I am not a bit sorry. I have loved unselfishly, and I have fondled hatred with the red-hot tongs of Hell. That's living.

I have no race prejudice of any kind. My kinfolks, and my "skinfolks" are dearly loved. My own circumference of every-day life is there. But I see their same virtues and vices every-where I look. So I give you all my right hand of fellowship and

love, and hope for the same from you. In my eyesight, you lose nothing by not looking just like me. I will remember you all in my good thoughts, and I ask you kindly to do the same for me. Not only just me. You who play the zig-zag lightning of power over the world, with the grumbling thunder in your wake, think kindly of those who walk in the dust. And you who walk in humble places, think kindly too, of others. There has been no proof in the world so far that you would be less arrogant if you held the lever of power in your hands. Let us all be kissing-friends. Consider that with tolerance and patience, we godly demons may breed a noble world in a few hundred generations or so. Maybe all of us who do not have the good fortune to meet or meet again, in this world, will meet at a barbecue.

APPENDIX
TO
DUST TRACKS ON A ROAD

"MY PEOPLE, MY PEOPLE!"

My People, My People!" This very minute, nations of people are moaning it and shaking their heads with a sigh. Thousands and millions of people are uttering it in different parts of the globe. Differences of geography and language make differences in sound, that's all. The sentiment is the same. Yet and still it is a private wail, sacred to my people.

Not that the expression is hard to hear. It is being thrown around with freedom. It is the interpretation that is difficult. No doubt hundreds of outsiders standing around have heard it often enough, but only those who have friended with us like Carl Van Vechten know what it means.

Which ever way you go to describe it—the cry, the sigh, the wail, the groaning grin or grinning groan of "My People, My People!" bursts from us when we see sights that bring on despair.

Say that a brown young woman, fresh from the classic halls of Barnard College and escorted by a black boy from Yale, enters the subway at 50th street. They are well-dressed, well-mannered and good to look at. The eyes of the entire coach agree on that. They are returning from a concert by Marian Anderson and are still vibrating from her glowing tones. They are saying happy things about the tribute the huge white audience paid her genius and her arts. Oh yes, they say, "the Race is going to amount to something after all. Definitely! Look at George W. Carver and Ernest Just and Abram Harris, and Barthe is getting on right well with his sculpture and E. Simms Campbell is holding his own on *Esquire* and oh yes, Charles S. Johnson isn't doing so badly either. Paul Robeson, E. Franklin Frazier, Roland Hayes, well you just take them for granted. There is hope indeed for the Race."

By that time the train pulls into 72nd street. Two scabby-looking Negroes come scrambling into the coach. The coach is not full. There are plenty of seats, but no matter how many vacant seats there are, no other place will do, except side by side with the Yale-Barnard couple. No, indeed! Being dirty and smelly, do they keep quiet otherwise? A thousand times, No! They woof, bookoo, broadcast and otherwise distriminate from one end of the coach to the other. They consider it a golden opportunity to put on a show. Everybody in the coach being new to them, they naturally have not heard about the way one of the pair beat his woman on Lenox Avenue. Therefore they must be told in great detail what led up to the fracas, how many teeth he knocked out during the fight, and what happened after. His partner is right there, isn't he? Well, all right now. He's in the conversation too, so he must talk out of his mouth and let the coach know just how he fixed *his* woman up when she tried that same on *him*.

Barnard and Yale sit there and dwindle and dwindle. They do not look around the coach to see what is in the faces of the white passengers. They know too well what is there. Some are grinning from the heel up and some are stonily quiet. But both kinds are thinking "That's just like a Negro." Not just like *some* Negroes, mind you, No, like all. Only difference is some Negroes are better dressed. Feeling all of this like rock-salt under the skin, Yale and Barnard shake their heads and moan "My People, My People!"

Maybe at the other end of the coach another couple are saying the same thing but with a different emotion. They say it with a chuckle. They have enjoyed the show, and they are

236

saying in the same tone of voice that a proud father uses when he boasts to others about that bad little boy of his at home. "Mischievous, into everything, beats up all the kids in the neighborhood. Don't know what I'm going to do with the little rascal." That's the way some folks say the thing.

Certain of My People have come to dread railway day coaches for this same reason. They dread such scenes more than they do the dirty upholstery and other inconveniences of a Jim Crow coach. They detest the forced grouping. The railroad company feels "you are all colored aren't you? So why not all together? If you are not all alike, *that's your own fault.* Once upon a time you were all alike. You had no business to change. If you are not that way, then it's just too bad. You're supposed to be like that." So when sensitive souls are forced to travel that way they sit there numb and when some free soul takes off his shoes and socks, they mutter "My race but not My taste." When somebody else eats fried fish, bananas and a mess of peanuts and throws all the leavings on the floor, they gasp "My skinfolks but not my kinfolks." And sadly over all, they keep sighing "My People, My People!"

Who are My People? I would say all those hosts spoken of as Negroes, Colored folks, Aunt Hagar's chillum, the brother in black, Race men and women, and My People. They range in color from Walter White, white through high yaller, yaller, Punkin color, high brown, vaseline brown, seal brown, black, smooth black, dusty black, rusty black, coal black, lam black and damn black. My people there in the south of the world, the east of the world, in the west and even some few in the north. Still and all, you can't just point out my people by skin color.

White people have come running to me with a deep wrinkle between the eyes asking me things. They have heard talk going around about this passing, so they are trying to get some information so they can know. So since I have been asked, that gives me leave to talk right out of my mouth.

In the first place, this passing business works both ways. All the passing is not passing for white. We have white folks

237

among us passing for colored. They just happened to be born with a tinge of brown in the skin and took up being colored as a profession. Take James Weldon Johnson for instance.

There's a man white enough to suit Hitler and he's been passing for colored for years.

Now, don't get the idea that he is not welcome among us. He certainly is. He has more than paid his way. But he just is not a Negro. You take a look at him and ask why I talk like that. But you know, I told you back there not to depend too much on skin. You'll certainly get mis-put on your road if you put too much weight on that. Look at James Weldon Johnson from head to foot, but don't let that skin color and that oskobolic hair fool you. Watch him! Does he parade when he walks? No, James Weldon Johnson proceeds. Did anybody ever, *ever* see him grin? No, he smiles. He couldn't give a grin if he tried. He can't even Uncle Tom. Not that I complain of "Tomming" if it's done right.

"Tomming" is not an aggressive act, it is true, but it has its uses like feinting in the prize ring. But James Weldon Johnson can't Tom. He has been seen trying it, but it was sad. Let him look around at some of the other large Negroes and hand over the dice.

No, I never expect to see James Weldon Johnson a success in the strictly Negro Arts, but I would not be at all surprised to see him crowned. The man is just full of that old monarch material. If some day I looked out of my window on Seventh Avenue and saw him in an ermine robe and a great procession going to the Cathedral of St. John the Divine to be crowned I wouldn't be a bit surprised. Maybe he'd make a mighty fine king at that. He's tried all he knew how to pass for colored, but he just hasn't made it. His own brother is scared in his presence. He bows and scrapes and calls him The Duke.

So now you say "Well, if you can't tell who My People are by skin color, how are you going to know?" There's more ways than one of telling, and I'm going to point them out right now.

Wait until you see a congregation of more than two dark complected people. If they can't agree on a single, solitary thing, then you can go off satisfied. Those are My People. It's just against nature for us to agree with each other. We not only refuse to agree, we'll get mad and fight about it. *But only each other!* Anybody else can cool us off right now. We fly hot quick, but we are easily cooled when we find out the person who made us mad is not another Negro.

There is the folk-tale of the white man who hired five men to take hold of a rope to pull up a cement block. They caught hold and gave a yank and the little stone flew way up to the pulley the first time. The men looked at one 'nother in surprise and so one of them said to the bossman: "Boss, how come you hire all of us to pull up that one little piece of rock? One man could do that by hisself." "Yeah, I know it," the bossman told him, "but I just wanted to see five Negroes pulling together once."

Then there is the story of the man who was called on to pray. He got down and he said "Oh Lord, I want to ask something, but I know you can't do it. I just *know* you can't do it." Then he took a long pause.

Somebody got restless and said "Go ahead and ask Him. That's God you talking to. He can do anything."

The man who was praying said "I know He is supposed to do all things, but this what I wants to ask. . . ."

"Aw go on and ask Him. God A'Mighty can do anything. Go on, brother, and ask Him and finish up your prayer."

"Well, alright, I'll ask Him. O Lord, I'm asking you because they tell me to go ahead. I'm asking you something, but I just know you can't do it. I just *know* you can't do it but I'll just ask you. Lord, I'm asking you to bring my people together, but I *know* you can't do it, Lord. Amen."

Maybe the Lord *can* do it, but he hasn't done it yet.

It do say in the Bible that the Lord started the disturbance himself. It was the sons of Ham who built the first big city and started the tower of Babel. They were singing and building their way to heaven when the Lord came down and confused their tongues. We haven't built no more towers and things like that but we still got the confusion. The other part about the building and what not may be just a folk-tale, but we've got proof about the tongue power.

So when you find a set of folks who won't agree on a thing, those are My People.

B

If you have your doubts, go and listen to the man. If he hunts for six big words where one little one would do, that's My People. If he can't find that big word he's feeling for, he is going to make a new one. But somehow or other that new-made word fits the thing it was made for. Sounds good, too. Take for instance the time when the man needed the word *slander* and he didn't know it. He just made the word distriminate and anybody that heard the word would know what he meant. "Don't distriminate de woman." Somebody didn't know the word total nor entire so they made bodacious. Then there's asterperious, and so on. When you find a man chewing up the dictionary and spitting out language, that's My People.

C

If you still have doubts, study the man and watch his ways. See if all of him fits into today. If he has no memory of yesterday, nor no concept of tomorrow, then he is My People. There is no tomorrow in the man. He mentions the word plentiful and often. But there is no real belief in a day that is not here and present. For him to believe in a tomorrow would mean an obligation to consequences. There is no sense of consequences. Else he is not My People.

D

If you are still not satisfied, put down two piles of money. Do not leave less than a thousand dollars in one pile and do not leave more than a dollar and a quarter in the other. Expose these two sums where they are equally easy to take. If he takes the thousand dollars he is not My People. That is settled. My People never steal more than a dollar and a quarter. This test is one of the strongest.

E

But the proof positive is the recognition of the monkey as our brother. No matter where you find the brother in black he is telling a story about his brother the monkey. Different languages and geography, but that same tenderness. There is recognition everywhere of the monkey as a brother. Whenever we want to poke a little fun at ourselves, we throw the cloak of our short-comings over the monkey. This is the American classic:

The monkey was playing in the road one day and a big new Cadillac come down the road full of white people. The driver saw the monkey and drove sort of to one side and went on. Several more cars came by and never troubled the monkey at all. Way after while here come long a Ford car full of Colored folks. The driver was showing off, washing his foot in the gas tank. The car could do 60 and he was doing 70 (he had the accelerator down to the floor). Instead of slowing up when he saw the monkey, he got faster and tried to run over him. The monkey just barely escaped by jumping way to one side. The Negro hollered at him and said, "Why de hell don't you git out of de way? You see me washing my feet in the gas tank! I ought to kill you." By that time they went on down the road. The monkey sat there and shook his head and said "My People, My People!" However, Georgette Harvey, that superb actress, said that she had spoken with our brother the monkey recently and he does not say "My People" any more. She says the last monkey she talked with was saying "Those People, Those People!" Maybe he done quit the Race. Walked out cold on the family.

F

If you look at a man and mistrust your eyes, do something and see if he will imitate you right away. If he does, that's My People. We love to imitate. We would rather do a good imitation than any amount of something original. Nothing is half so good as something that is just like something else. And no title is so coveted as the "black this or that." Roland Hayes is right white folksy that way. He has pointedly refused the title of "The Black Caruso." It's got to be Roland Hayes or nothing. But he is exceptional that way. We have Black Patti, Black Yankees, Black Giants. Rose McClendon was referred to time and again as the Black Barrymore. Why we even had a Black Dillinger! He was the Negro that Dillinger carried out of Crown Point when he made his famous wooden gun escape. Of course he didn't last but a day or two after he got back to Detroit or Buffalo, or where ever he was before the police gave him a black-out. He could have kept quiet and lived a long time perhaps, but he would rather risk dying than to miss wearing his title. As far as he was able, he was old Dillinger himself. Julian, the parachute jumper, risked his life by falling in the East River pretending he knew how to run an aeroplane like Lindbergh to gain his title of Black Eagle. Lindbergh landed in Paris and Julian landed in New-York harbor, but, anyhow, he flew some.

What did Haiti ever do to make the world glad it happened? Well, they held a black revolution right behind the white one in France. And now their Senators and Deputies go around looking like cartoons of French Ministers and Senators in spade whiskers and other goatee forms. They wave their hands and arms and explain about their latin temperaments, but it is not impressive. If you didn't hear them talk, in a bunch, they

242

could be Adam Powell's Abbysinia Baptist Church turning out and nobody would know the difference.

In Jamaica, the various degrees of Negroes put on some outward show to impress you that no matter what your eyes tell you, that they are really white folks—*white* English folks inside. The moment you meet a mulatto there he makes an opportunity to tell you who his father was. You are bound to hear a lot about that Englishman or that Scot. But never a word about the black mama. It is as if she didn't exist. Had never existed at all. You get the impression that Jamaica is the place where roosters lay eggs. That these Englishmen come there and without benefit of females they just scratch out a nest and lay an egg that hatches out a Jamaican.

As badly as the Ethiopians hated to part with Haile Selassie and freedom, it must be some comfort to have Mussolini for a model. By now, all the Rasses and other big shots are tootching out their lips ferociously, gritting their teeth and otherwise making faces like Il Duce. And I'll bet you a fat man against sweet back that all the little boy Ethiopians are doing a mean pouter pigeon strut around Addis Ababa.

And right here in these United States, we don't miss doing a thing that the white folks do, possible or impossible. Education, Sports, keeping up with the Joneses and the whole shebang. The unanswerable retort to criticism is "The white folks do it, don't they?" In Mobile, Alabama, I saw the Millionaires' ball. A man who roomed in the same house with me got me a ticket and carried me to a seat in the balcony. He warned me not to come down on the dance floor until the first dance was over. The Millionaires and their lady friends would want the floor all to themselves for that dance. It was very special. I was duly impressed, I tell you.

The ball opened with music. A fairly good dance orchestra was on the job. That first dance, exclusively for the Millionaires, was announced and each Millionaire and his lady friend were announced by name as they took the floor.

"John D. Rockefeller, dancing with Miss Selma Jones!" I looked down and out walked Mr. Rockefeller in a pair of white wool pants with a black pin stripe, pink silk shirt without a coat because it was summer time. Ordinarily, Mr. Rockefeller delivered hats for a millinery shop, but not tonight.

Commodore Vanderbilt was announced and took the floor. The Commodore was so thin in his ice-cream pants that he just had no behind at all. Mr. Ford pranced out with his lady doing a hot cut-out. J. P. Morgan entered doing a mean black-bottom, and so on. Also each Millionaire presented his lady friend with a five-dollar gold piece after the dance. It was reasoned the Millionaires would have done the same for the same pleasure.

G

Last but not least, My People love a show. We love to act more than we love to see acting done. We love to look at them and we love to put them on, and we love audiences when we get to specifying. That's why some of us take advantage of trains and other public places like dance halls and picnics. We just love to dramatize.

Now you've been told, so you ought to know. But maybe, after all the Negro doesn't really exist. What we think is a race is detached moods and phases of other people walking around. What we have been talking about might not exist at all. Could be the shade patterns of something else thrown on the ground—other folks, seen in shadow. And even if we do exist it's all an accident anyway. God made everybody else's color. We took ours by mistake. The way the old folks tell it, it was like this, you see.

God didn't make people all of a sudden. He made folks by degrees. First he stomped out the clay and then he cut out the patterns and propped 'em against the fence to dry. Then after they was dry, He took and blowed the breath of life into 'em and sent 'em on off. Next day He told everybody to come up and get toe-nails. So everybody come and got their toe-nails and finger-nails and went on off. Another time He said for everybody to come get their Nose and Mouth because He

244

was giving 'em out that day. So everybody come got noses and mouths and went on off. Kept on like that till folks had everything but their color. So one day God called everybody up and said, "Now I want everybody around the throne at seven o'clock sharp tomorrow morning. I'm going to give out color tomorrow morning and I want everybody here on time. I got a lot more creating to do and I want to give out this color and be through with that."

Seven o'clock next morning God was sitting on His throne with His great crown on His head. He looked North, He looked East, He looked West and He looked Australia and blazing worlds was falling off of His teeth. After a while He looked down from His high towers of elevation and considered the Multitudes in front of Him. He looked to His left and said, "Youse red people!" so they all turned red and said "Thank you, God" and they went on off. He looked at the next host and said, "Youse yellow people!" and they got yellow and said "Thank you, God" and they went on off. Then He looked at the next multitude and said, "Youse white people" and they got white and told Him, "Thank you, God" and they went on off. God looked on His other hand and said, "Gabriel, look like I miss some hosts." Gabriel looked all around and said, "Yes, sir, several multitudes ain't here." "Well," God told him, "you go hunt 'em up and tell 'em I say they better come quick if they want any color. Fool with me and I won't give out no more." So Gabriel went round everywhere hunting till way after while he found the lost multitudes down by the Sea of Life asleep under a tree. So he told them they better hurry if they wanted any color. God wasn't going to wait on them much longer. So everybody jumped up and went running up to the throne. When the first ones got there they couldn't stop because the ones behind kept on pushing and shoving. They kept on until the throne was careening way over to one side. So God hollered at 'em "Get back! Get back!!" But they thought He said "Git black!" So they got black and just kept the thing agoing.

So according to that, we are no race. We are just a collection of people who overslept our time and got caught in the draft.

ZORA NEALE HURSTON
July 2, 1937
Port-au-Prince, Haiti.

SEEING THE WORLD
AS IT IS

❖

Thing lies forever in her birthing-bed and glories. But hungry Time squats beside her couch and waits. His frame was made out of emptiness, and his mouth set wide for prey. Mystery is his oldest son, and power is his portion.

That brings me before the unlived hour, that first mystery of the Universe with its unknown face and reflecting back. For it was said on the day of first sayings that Time should speak backward over his shoulder, and none should see his face, so scornful is he of the creatures of Thing.

What the faceless years will do to me, I do not know. I see Time's footprints, and I gaze into his reflections. My knees have dragged the basement of Hell and I have been in Sorrow's Kitchen, and it has seemed to me that I have licked out all the pots. The winters have been and my soul-stuff has lain mute like a plain while the herds of happenings thundered across my breast. In these times there were deep chasms in me which had forgotten their memory of the sun.

But time has his beneficent moods. He has commanded some servant-moments to transport me to high towers of elevation so that I might look out on the breadth of things. This is a privilege granted to a servant of many hours, but a master of few, from the master of a trillion billion hours and the servant of none.

In those moments I have seen that it is futile for me to seek the face of, and fear, an accusing God withdrawn somewhere beyond the stars in space. I myself live upon a star, and I can be satisfied with the millions of assurances of deity about me. If I have not felt the divinity of man in his cults, I have found it in his works. When I lift my eyes to the towering structures of Manhattan, and look upon the mighty tunnels and bridges of the world, I know that my search is over, and that I can depart in peace. For my soul tells me, "Truly this is the son of God. The rocks and the winds, the tides and the hills are his servants. If he talks in finger-rings, he works in horizons which dwarf the equator. His works are as noble as his words are foolish."

I found that I had no need of either class or race prejudice, those scourges of humanity. The solace of easy generalization was taken from me, but I received the richer gift of individualism. When I have been made to suffer or when I have been made happy by others, I have known that individuals were responsible for that, and not races. All clumps of people turn out to be individuals on close inspection.

This has called for a huge cutting of dead wood on my part. From my earliest remembrance, I heard the phrases, "Race Problem," "Race Pride," "Race Man or Woman," "Race Solidarity," "Race Consciousness," "Race Leader," and the like. It was a point of pride to be pointed out as a "Race Man." And to say to one, "Why, you are not a race man," was low-rating a person. Of course these phrases were merely sounding syllables to me as a child. Then the time came when I thought they meant something. I cannot say that they ever really came clear in my mind, but they probably were as clear to me as they were to the great multitude who uttered them. Now, they mean nothing to me again. At least nothing that I want to feel.

There could be something wrong with me because I see Negroes neither better nor worse than any other race. Race pride is a luxury I cannot afford. There are too many implications behind the term. Now, suppose a Negro does something really magnificent, and I glory, not in the benefit to mankind, but in the fact that the doer was a Negro. Must I not also go hang my head in shame when a member of my race does something execrable? If I glory, then the obligation is laid upon me to blush also. I *do* glory when a Negro does something fine, I gloat because he or she has done a fine thing, but not because he was a Negro. That is incidental and accidental. It is the human achievement which I honor. I execrate a foul act of a Negro but again not on the grounds that the doer was a Negro, but because it was foul. A member of my race just happened to be the fouler of humanity. In other words, I know that I cannot accept responsibility for thirteen million people. Every tub must sit on its own bottom regardless. So "Race Pride" in me had to go. And anyway, why should I be proud to be a Negro? Why should anybody be proud to be white? Or yellow? Or red? After all, the word "race" is a loose classification of physical characteristics. It tells nothing about the insides of people. Pointing at achievements tells nothing either. Races have never done anything. What seems race achievement is the work of individuals. The white race did not go into a laboratory and invent incandescent light. That was Edison. The Jews did not work out Relativity. That was Einstein. The Negroes did not find out the inner secrets of peanuts and sweet potatoes, nor the secret of the development of the egg. That was Carver and Just. If you are under the impression that every white man is an Edison, just look around a bit. If you have the idea that every Negro is a Carver, you had better take off plenty of time to do your searching.

No, instead of Race Pride being a virtue, it is a sapping vice. It has caused more suffering in the world than religious opinion, and that is saying a lot.

"Race Conscious" is about the same as Race Pride in meaning. But, granting the shade of difference, all you say for it is, "Be continually conscious of what race you belong to so you can be proud." That is the effect of the thing. But what use is that? I don't care which race you belong to. If you are only one quarter honest in your judgment, you can seldom be proud. Why waste time keeping conscious of your physical aspects? What the world is crying and dying for at this moment is less race consciousness. The human race would blot itself out entirely if it had any more. It is a deadly explosive on the tongues of men. I choose to forget it.

This Race Problem business, now. I have asked many well-educated people of both races to tell me what the problem is. They look startled at first. Then I can see them scratching around inside themselves hunting for the meaning of the words which they have used with so much glibness and unction. I have never had an answer that was an answer, so I have had to make up my own. Since there is no fundamental conflict, since there is no solid reason why the blacks and the whites cannot live in one nation in perfect harmony, the only thing in the way of it is Race Pride and Race Consciousness on both sides. A bear has been grabbed by the tail. The captor and the captured are walking around a tree snarling at each other. The man is scared to turn the bear loose, and his hand-hold is slipping. The bear wants to go on about his business, but he feels that something must be done about that tail-hold. So they just keep on following each other around the tree.

So Race Pride and Race Consciousness seem to me to be not only fallacious, but a thing to be abhorred. It is the root of misunderstanding and hence misery and injustice. I cannot, with logic cry against it in others and wallow in it myself. The only satisfaction to be gained from it anyway is, "I ain't nothing, my folks ain't nothing, but that makes no difference at all. I belong to such-and-such a race." Poor nourishment according to my notion. Mighty little to chew on. You have to season it awfully high with egotism to make it tasty.

Priding yourself on your physical make up, something over which you have no control, is just another sign that the human cuss is determined not to be grateful. He gives himself a big hand on the way he looks and lets on that he arranged it all himself. God got suspicious that he was going to be like that before He made him, and that is why Old Maker caught up on all of His creating before He made Man. He knew that if Man had seen how He did it, just as soon as a woman came along to listen to him, Man would have been saying, "See that old striped tiger over there? *I* made him. Turned him out one morning before breakfast." And so on until there would not have been a thing in Heaven or earth that he didn't take credit for. So God did the only thing he could to narrow down the field for boasting. He made him late and kept him dumb.

And how can Race Solidarity be possible in a nation made up of as many elements as these United States? It could result in nothing short of chaos. The fate of each and every group is bound up with the others. Individual ability in any group must function for all the rest. National disaster touches us all. There is no escape in grouping. And in practice there can be no sharp lines drawn, because the interest of every individual in any racial group is not identical with the others. Section, locality, self-interest, special fitness, and the like set one group of Anglo-Saxons, Jews, and Negroes against another set of Anglo-Saxons, Jews, and Negroes. We are influenced by a pain in the pocket just like everybody else. During the Civil War Negroes fought in the Confederate Army because many Negroes were themselves slave-owners, and were just as mad at Lincoln as anybody else in the South. Anybody who goes before a body and purports to plead for what "The Negro" wants, is a liar and knows it. Negroes want a variety of things and many of them diametrically opposed. There is no single Negro nor no single organization which can carry the thirteen million in any direction. Even Joe Louis can't do it, but he comes nearer to it than anyone else at present.

And why should Negroes be united? Nobody else in America is. If it were true, then one of two other things would be true. One, that they were united on what the white people are united on, and it would take a God to tell what that is; and be moving towards complete and immediate assimilation. Or we would be united on something specially Negroid, and that would lead towards a hard black knot in the body politic which would be impossible of place in the nation. All of the upper class Negroes certainly want political and economic equality. That is the most universal thing I can pin down.

Negroes are just like anybody else. Some soar. Some plod ahead. Some just make a mess and step back in it—like the rest of America and the world. So Racial Solidarity is a fiction and always will be. Therefore, I have lifted the word out of my mouth.

A Race Man is somebody, not necessarily able, who places his race before all else. He says he will buy everything from a Negro merchant as far as possible, support all "race" institutions and movements and so on. The only thing that keeps this from working is that it is impossible to form a nation within a nation. He makes spurts and jerks at it, but every day he is forced away from it by necessity. He finds that he can neither make money nor spend money in a restricted orbit. He is part of the national economy. But he can give the idea plenty of talk. He springs to arms over such things as the title of Carl Van Vechten's book, *Nigger Heaven,* or Will Rogers saying over the radio that most of the cowboy songs were nothing more than adaptations of "nigger tunes." He does this because he feels that he is defending his race. Sometimes the causes are just, and sometimes they are ridiculous. His zeal is honest enough; it is merely a lack of analysis that leads him into error.

As I said before, the Race Leader is a fiction that is good only at the political trough. But it is not nearly so good as it used to be. The white political leaders have found out more or less that they cannot deliver wholesale. Many of them are successful in a way, but not in any great, big, plushy way. The politician may try ever so hard, but, if people won't follow, he just can't lead. Being an American, I am just like the rest of the Yankees, the Westerners, the Southerners, the Negroes, the Irish, the Indians, and the Jews. I don't lead well either. Don't just tell me what to do. Tell me what is being contemplated and let me help figure on the bill. That is my idea, and I am going to stick to it. Negroes are so much like the rest of

America that they not only question what is put before them, but they have got so they order something else besides gin at the bars, which is certainly a sign of something. So I have thrown over the idea of Race Leadership, too.

I know that there is race prejudice, not only in America, but also wherever two races meet together in numbers. I have met it in the flesh, and I have found out that it is never all on one side, either. I do not give it heart room because it seems to me to be the last refuge of the weak. From what little I have been able to learn, I know that goodness, ability, vice, and dumbness know nothing about race lives or geography. I do not wish to close the frontiers of life upon my own self. I do not wish to deny myself the expansion of seeking into individual capabilities and depths by living in a space whose boundaries are race and nation. Lord, give my poor stammering tongue at least one taste of the whole round world, if you please, Sir.

And then I know so well that the people who make a boast of racial, class, or national prejudices do so out of a sense of incapability to which they refuse to give a voice. Instead they try to be ingenious by limiting competition. They are racial card-sharks trying to rig the game so that they cannot lose. Trying to stack the deck. If I choose to call these card-palmers poor sports, then the burden of proof is on them. I give the matter the corner of my eye and smile at the back-hand compliment, for I know that if I had been born where *they* were born, and they had been born where *I* was born, it is hardly likely that we ever would have met. So I smile and not bitterly, either. For I know that Equality is as you do it and not as you talk it. If you are better than I, you can tell me about it if you want to, but then again, show me so I can know. It is always good to be learning something. But if you never make me know it, I'll keep on questioning. I love to be in the presence of my superiors. If I don't catch on right away, crumble it up fine so I can handle it. And then again, if you can't *show* me your superiority, don't bother to bring the mess up, lest I merely rate you as a bully.

Since I wash myself of race pride and repudiate race solidar-

253

ity, by the same token I turn my back upon the past. I see no reason to keep my eyes fixed on the dark years of slavery and the Reconstruction. I am three generations removed from it, and therefore have no experience of the thing. From what I can learn, it was sad. No doubt America would have been better off if it never had been. But it was and there is no use in beating around the bush. Still, there seems to me to be nothing but futility in gazing backward over my shoulder and buking the grave of some white man who has been dead too long to talk about. Neither do I see any use in button-holing his grandson about it. The old man probably did cut some capers back there, and I'll bet you anything my old folks didn't like it. But the old man is dead. My old folks are dead. Let them wrestle all over Hell about it if they want to. That is their business. The present is upon me and that white man's grand-children as well. I have business with the grandson as of today. I want to get on with the business in hand. Since I cannot pry loose the clutching hand of time, I will settle for some influ-ence on the present. It is ridiculous for me to make out that I'm Old Black Joe and waste my time rehashing his problems. That would be just as ridiculous as it would be for the Jews to hang around the pyramids trying to get a word with Old Cheops. Or for the English to be billing the Duke of Nor-mandy the first of every month.

I am all for starting something brand new in co-operation with the present incumbent. If I don't get any co-operation, I am going to start something anyway. The world is not just going to stand still looking like a fool at a funeral if I can help it. Let's bring up right now and lay a hearing on it.

Standing on the watch-wall and looking, I no longer expect the millennium. It would be wishful thinking to be searching for justice in the absolute. People are not made so it will happen, because from all I can see, the world is a whole family of Hurstons. It has always been a family of Hurstons, so it is foolish to expect any justice untwisted by the selfish hand. Look into the Book of Books and it is not even there. The Old Testament is devoted to what was right and just from the viewpoint of the Ancient Hebrews. All of their enemies were twenty-two carat evil. They, the Hebrews, were never aggressors. The Lord wanted His children to have a country full of big grapes and tall corn. Incidentally while they were getting it, they might as well get rid of some trashy tribes that He never did think much of, anyway. With all of its figs and things, Canaan was their destiny. God sent somebody especially to tell them about it. If the conquest looked like bloody rape to the Canaanites, that was because their evil ways would not let them see a point which was right under their nose. So you had to drive it in under the ribs. King David, who invented the "protection" racket in those days before he was saved by being made king, was a great hero. He only killed and pillaged to help out his own folks. He was a man after God's own heart, and was quite serviceable in helping God get rid of no-count rascals who were cluttering up the place.

The New Testament is not quite so frank but it is equally biased. Paul and the disciples set up a New Order in Palestine after the death of Jesus, but the Jews gave it nothing but their shoulder-blades. So now, the Orthodox Jew became a manifest enemy of right. To this day, the names of Pharisee and Sadducee are synonymous with hypocrite and crook to ninety-nine and a half percent of the Christian world. While in fact, the Pharisee was an order small in number, highly educated, well born, and clean living men whose mission was to guard the purity of the creed. The Sadducees were almost as lofty. Naturally in the turmoil of the times, they got embroiled in politics in the very nature of the form of their government, but so have both branches of Christianity.

Then there is the slaughter of the innocents by Herod. One thing strikes me curious about that slaughter. The unconverted Jews never seemed to have missed their babies. So Herod must have carefully selected babies from families who forty years later were going to turn Christian. He probably did not realize what a bad example he was setting for the new religionists. He could not have known that centuries later

Christians would themselves slaughter more innocents in one night than his soldiers ever saw.

Those Jews who would not accept Christianity look very bad in the New Testament. And two thousand years have gone by and all the Western World uses the sign of the Cross, but it is evident that the Jews are not the only ones who do not accept it. The Occident has never been christianized and never will be. It is an oriental concept which the sons of hammer-throwing Thor have no enzymes to digest. It calls for meekness, and the West is just not made meek. Instead of being proud to turn the other cheek, our boast is beating the other fellow to the punch.

We have even turned the Gospel of peace into a wrestle, we club each other over the head to prove who is the best missionary. Nature asserts itself. We can neither give up our platitudes nor our profits. The platitudes sound beautiful, but the profits feel like silk.

Popes and Prelates, Bishops and Elders have halted sermons on peace at the sound of battle and rushed out of their pulpits brandishing swords and screaming for blood in Jesus' name. The pews followed the pulpit in glee. So it is obvious that the Prince of Peace is nothing more than a symbol. He has been drafted into every army in the Occident. He must have a delegate behind every cannon. We have tangled with the soft and yielding thing for twenty long centuries without any more progress than letting the words take up around the house. We are moral enough, just not Christians. If we love meekness as we say, then Napoleon should be pictured in a nun's robe, Bismarck in a cassock and George Washington in a Gandhi diaper. The pedestals should read "These stones do honor to our meekest men. Their piety laid millions low. Praise the Lord!" The actual representation would reveal the confusion in our minds. According to our worship, Joe Louis rates a Cardinal's hat.

But back to Mahatma Gandhi. His application of Christian principles is causing us great distress. We want the people to hear about it from Greenland's icy mountains, to India's coral

256

strand, but we do wish that they would not lose their heads and carry the thing too far, like Gandhi does for instance. It is a bad thing for business.

No, actual justice is somewhere away off. We only see its flickering image here. Everybody has it on his tongue and nobody has it at heart. Take, for instance, the matter of conquest.

The Kings of Dahomey once marched up and down West Africa, butchering the aged and the helpless of the surrounding tribes and nations, and selling the able off into Western slavery. The Dahomans would have been outraged if anybody had said they were unjust. What could be more just? The profits were enormous. But they did feel that there was no more justice in the world when the French came in and conquered them. The French would have shrugged down the Pyramids if they had been told that they were not just. What could be fairer? The Germans have now conquered the French and the French wonder how those Germans can be so lacking in soul. But the Germans open their blue eyes in amazement. Why, nothing could be more reasonable and just. If the world cannot find pure justice among the Germans, they will never find it anywhere. If the French want to be unfair enough to begrudge them their little profit on the deal, it shows how narrow and mean-minded a Frenchman really can be.

There is no diffused light on anything international so that a comparatively whole scene may be observed. Light is sharply directed on one spot, leaving not only the greater part in darkness but also denying by implication that the great unlighted field exists. It is no longer profitable, with few exceptions, to ask people what they think, for you will be told what they wish, instead. Perhaps at no other period in the history of the world have people lived in such a dreamy state. People even waste time denouncing their enemies in open warfare for shooting back too hard, or too accurately. There is no attempt to be accurate as to truth, however. The whole idea is to be complimentary to one's self and keep alive the dream. The other man's side commits gross butcheries. One's own side wins smashing victories.

Being human and a part of humanity, I like to think that my own nation is more just than any other in spite of the facts on hand. It makes me feel prouder and bigger to think that way. But now and then the embroidered hangings blow aside, and I am less exalted. I see that the high principles enunciated so throatedly are like the flowers in spring—they have nothing to do with the case. If my conclusions are in error, then the orators and copy-books were wrong to start off with. I should have been told in the very beginning that those were words to copy, but not to go by. But they didn't tell me that. They swore by jeepers and by joe that there were certain unshakable truths that no man nor nation could make out without.

There was the dignity of man. His inalienable rights were sacred. Man, noble man, had risen in his might and glory and had stamped out the vile institution of slavery. That is just what they said. But I know that the principle of human bondage has not yet vanished from the earth. I know that great nations are standing on it. I would not go so far as to deny that there has been no progress toward the concept of liberty. Already it has been agreed that the name of slavery is very bad. No civilized nation will use such a term anymore. Neither will they keep the business around the home. Life will be on a loftier level by operating at a distance and calling it acquiring sources of raw material, and keeping the market open. It has been decided also, that it is not cricket to enslave one's own kind. That is unspeakable tyranny.

But must a nation suffer from lack of prosperity and expansion by lofty concepts? Not at all! If a ruler can find a place way off where the people do not look like him, kill enough of them to convince the rest that they ought to support him with their lives and labor, that ruler is hailed as a great conqueror, and people build monuments to him. The very weapons he used are also honored. They picture him in unforgetting stone with the sacred tool of his conquest in his hand.

258

Democracy, like religion, never was designed to make our profits less.

Now, for instance, if the English people were to quarter troops in France, and force the French to work for them for forty-eight cents a week while they took more than a billion dollars a year out of France, the English would be Occidentally execrated. But actually, the British Government does just that in India, to the glory of the democratic way. They are hailed as not only great Empire builders, the English are extolled as leaders of civilization. And the very people who claim that it is a noble thing to die for freedom and democracy cry out in horror when they hear tell of a "revolt" in India. They even wax frothy if anyone points out the inconsistency of their morals. So this life as we know it is a great thing. It would have to be, to justify certain things.

I do not mean to single England out as something strange and different in the world. We, too, have our Marines in China. We, too, consider machine gun bullets good laxatives for heathens who get constipated with toxic ideas about a country of their own. If the patient dies from the treatment, it was not because the medicine was not good. We are positive of that. We have seen it work on other patients twice before it killed them and three times after. Then, too, no matter what the outcome, you have to give the doctor credit for trying.

The United States being the giant of the Western World, we have our responsibilities. The little Latin brother south of the border has been a trifle trying at times. Nobody doubts that he means to be a good neighbor. We know that his intentions are the best. It is only that he is so gay and fiesta-minded that he is liable to make arrangements that benefit nobody but himself. Not a selfish bone in his body, you know. Just too full of rumba. So it is our big brotherly duty to teach him right from wrong. He must be taught to share with big brother before big brother comes down and kicks his teeth in. A big *good* neighbor is a lovely thing to have. We are far too moral a people to allow poor Latin judgment to hinder good works.

But there is a geographical boundary to our principles.

They are not to leave the United States unless we take them ourselves. Japan's application of our principles to Asia is never to be sufficiently deplored. We are like the southern planter's bride when he kissed her the first time.

"Darling," she fretted, "do niggers hug and kiss like this?"

"Why, I reckon they do, honey. Fact is, I'm sure of it. Why do you ask?"

"You go right out and kill the last one of 'em tomorrow morning. Things like this is much too good for niggers."

Our indignation is more than justified. We Westerners composed that piece about trading in China with gunboats and cannons long decades ago. Japan is now plagiarizing in the most flagrant manner. We also wrote that song about keeping a whole hemisphere under your wing. Now the Nipponese are singing our song all over Asia. They are full of stuff and need a good working out. The only holdback to the thing is that they have copied our medicine chest. They are stocked up with the same steel pills and cannon plasters that Doctor Occident prescribes.

Mexico, the dear little papoose, has been on the sick list, too. Gangrene had set in in the upper limbs, so to speak, and amputation was the only thing which could save the patient. Even so, the patient malingered for a long time, and internal dosage had to be resorted to on occasion. The doctor is not sure that all of the germs have been eradicated from the system as yet, but, when the patient breaks out of the hospital, what can the doctor do?

In great and far-sighted magnanimity, no cases have been overlooked. The African tribesmen were saved from the stuffiness of overweening pride and property just in the nick of time.

Looking at all these things, I am driven to the conclusion that democracy is a wonderful thing, but too powerful to be trusted in any but purely occidental hands. Asia and Africa should know about it. They should die for it in defense of its originators, but they must not use it themselves.

All around me, bitter tears are being shed over the fate of

Holland, Belgium, France, and England. I must confess to being a little dry around the eyes. I hear people shaking with shudders at the thought of Germany collecting taxes in Holland. I have not heard a word against Holland collecting one twelfth of poor people's wages in Asia. That makes the ruling families in Holland very rich, as they should be. What happens to the poor Javanese and Balinese is unimportant; Hitler's crime is that he is actually doing a thing like that to his own kind. That is international cannibalism and should be stopped. He is a bandit. That is true, but that is not what is held against him. He is muscling in on well-established mobs. Give him credit. He cased some joints away off in Africa and Asia, but the big mobs already had them paying protection money and warned him to stay away. The only way he can climb out of the punk class is to high-jack the load and that is just what he is doing. President Roosevelt could extend his four freedoms to some people right here in America before he takes it all aboard, and, no doubt, he would do it too, if it would bring in the same amount of glory. I am not bitter, but I see what I see. He can call names across an ocean, but he evidently has not the courage to speak even softly at home. Take away the ocean and he simmers right down. I wish that I could say differently, but I cannot. I will fight for my country, but I will not lie for her. Our country is so busy playing "fence" to the mobsters that the cost in human suffering cannot be considered yet. We can take that up in the next depression.

As I see it, the doctrines of democracy deal with the aspirations of men's souls, but the application deals with things. One hand in somebody else's pocket and one on your gun, and you are highly civilized. Your heart is where it belongs—in your pocket-book. Put it in your bosom and you are backward. Desire enough for your own use only, and you are a heathen. Civilized people have things to show to the neighbors.

This is not to say, however, that the darker races are visiting angels, just touristing around here below. They have acted the same way when they had a chance and will act that way again, comes the break. I just think it would be a good thing for the

Anglo-Saxon to get the idea out of his head that everybody else owes him something just for being blonde. I am forced to the conclusion that two-thirds of them do hold that view. The idea of human slavery is so deeply ground in that the pink-toes can't get it out of their system. It has just been decided to move the slave quarters farther away from the house. It would be a fine thing if on leaving office, the blond brother could point with pride to the fact that his administration had done away with group-profit at the expense of others. I know well that it has never happened before, but it could happen, couldn't it?

To mention the hundred years of the Anglo-Saxon in China alone is proof enough of the evils of this view point. The millions of Chinese who have died for our prestige and profit! They are still dying for it. Justify it with all the proud and pretty phrases you please, but if we think our policy is right, you just let the Chinese move a gunboat in the Hudson to drum up trade with us. The scream of outrage would wake up saints in the backrooms of Heaven. And what is worse, we go on as if the so-called inferior people are not thinking; or if they do, it does not matter. As if no day could ever come when that which went over the Devil's back will buckle under his belly. People may not be well-armed at present, but you can't stop them from thinking.

I do not brood, however, over the wide gaps between ideals and practices. The world is too full of inconsistencies for that. I recognize that men are given to handling words long before those words have any internal meaning for them. It is as if we were children playing in a field and found something round and hard to play with. It may be full of beauty and pleasure, and then again it may be full of death.

And now to another matter. Many people have pointed out to me that I am a Negro, and that I am poor. Why then have I not joined a party of protest? I will tell you why. I see many good points in, let us say, the Communist Party. Anyone would be a liar and a fool to claim that there was no good in it. But I am so put together that I do not have much of a herd

262

instinct. Or if I must be connected with the flock, let *me* be the shepherd my ownself. That is just the way I am made.

You cannot arouse any enthusiasm in me to join in a protest for the boss to provide me with a better hoe to chop his cotton with. Why must I chop cotton at all? Why fix a class of cotton-choppers? I will join in no protests for the boss to put a little more stuffing in my bunk. I don't even want the bunk. I want the boss's bed. It seems to me that the people who are enunciating these principles are so saturated with European ideas that they miss the whole point of America. The people who founded this country, and the immigrants who came later, came here to get away from class distinctions and to keep their unborn children from knowing about them. I am all for the idea of free vertical movement, nothing horizontal. Let him who can, go up, and him who cannot stay there, mount down to the level his capabilities rate. It works out that way anyhow, hence the saying from shirt-sleeves to shirt-sleeves in three generations. The able at the bottom always snatch the ladder from under the weak on the top rung. That is the way it should be. A dead grandfather's back has proven to be a poor prop time and time again. If they have gone up there and stayed, they had something more than a lucky ancestor. So I can get no lift out of nominating myself to be a peasant and celebrating any feasts back stairs. I want the front of the house and I am going to keep on trying even if I never satisfy my plan.

Then, too, it seems to me that if I say a whole system must be upset for me to win, I am saying that I cannot sit in the game, and that safer rules must be made to give me a chance. I repudiate that. If others are in there, deal me a hand and let me see what I can make of it, even though I know some in there are dealing from the bottom and cheating like hell in other ways. If I can win anything in a game like that, I know I'll end up with the pot if the sharks can be eliminated. As the Negroes say down south, "You can't beat me and my prayers," and they are not talking about supplications either when they talk like that. I don't want to bother with any boring from within. If the leaders on the left feel that only violence can right things, I see no need of finger-nail warfare. Why not take a stronger position? Shoot in the hearse, don't care how sad the funeral is. Get the feeling of the bantam hen jumping on the mule. Kill dead and go to jail. I am not bloodthirsty and have no yearning for strife, but if what they say is true, that there must be this upset, why not make it cosmic? A lot of people would join in for the drama of it, who would not be moved by guile.

I do not say that my conclusions about anything are true for the Universe, but I have lived in many ways, sweet and bitter, and they feel right for me. I have seen and heard. I have sat in judgment upon the ways of others, and in the voiceless quiet of the night I have also called myself to judgment. I cannot have the joy of knowing that I found always a shining reflection of honor and wisdom in the mirror of my soul on those occasions. I have given myself more harrowing pain than anyone else has ever been capable of giving me. No one else can inflict the hurt of faith unkept. I have had the corroding insight at times of recognizing that I am a bundle of sham and tinsel, honest metal and sincerity that cannot be untangled. My dross has given my other parts great sorrow.

But, on the other hand, I have given myself the pleasure of sunrises blooming out of oceans, and sunsets drenching heaped-up clouds. I have walked in storms with a crown of clouds about my head and the zig zag lightning playing through my fingers. The gods of the upper air have uncovered their faces to my eyes. I have made friends with trees and vales. I have found out that my real home is in the water, that the earth is only my step-mother. My old man, the Sun, sired me out of the sea.

Like all mortals, I have been shaped by the chisel in the hand of Chance—bulged out here by a sense of victory, shrunken there by the press of failure and the knowledge of unworthiness. But it has been given to me to strive with life, and to conquer the fear of death. I have been correlated to the world so that I know the indifference of the sun to human emotions. I know that destruction and construction are but two faces of

Dame Nature, and that it is nothing to her if I choose to make personal tragedy out of her unbreakable laws.

So I ask of her few things. May I never do good consciously, nor evil unconsciously. Let my evil be known to me in advance of my acts, and my good when Nature wills. May I be granted a just mind and a timely death.

While I am still far below the allotted span of time, and notwithstanding, I feel that I have lived. I have the joy and pain of strong friendships. I have served and been served. I have made enemies of which I am not ashamed. I have been faithless, and then I have been faithful and steadfast until the blood ran down into my shoes. I have loved unselfishly with all the ardor of a strong heart, and I have hated with all the power of my soul. What waits for me in the future? I do not know. I cannot even imagine, and I am glad for that. But already, I have touched the four corners of the horizon, for from hard searching it seems to me that tears and laughter, love and hate, make up the sum of life.

THE INSIDE LIGHT—BEING
A SALUTE TO FRIENDSHIP

❖

Now take friendship for instance. It is a wonderful trade, a noble thing for anyone to work at. God made the world out of tough things, so it could last, and then He made some juice out of the most interior and best things that He had and poured it around for flavor.

You see lonesome-looking old red hills who do not even have clothes to cover their backs just lying there looking useless. Looking just like Old Maker had a junk pile like everybody else. But go back and look at them late in the day and see the herd of friendly shadows browsing happily around the feet of those hills. Then gaze up at the top and surprise the departing sun, all colored-up with its feelings, saying a sweet good night to those lonesome hills, and making them a promise that he will never forget them. So much tender beauty in a parting must mean a friendship. "I will visit you with my love," says the sun. That is why the hills endure.

Personally, I know what it means. I have never been as good a friend as I meant to be. I keep seeing new heights and depths of possibilities which ought to be reached, only to be frustrated by the press of life which is no friend to grace. I have my loyalties and my unselfish acts to my credit, but I feel the lack of perfection in them, and it leaves a hunger in me.

But I have received unaccountable friendship that is satisfying. Such as I am, I am a precious gift, as the unlettered Negro would say it. Stripped to my skin, that is just what I am. Without the juice of friendship, I would not be even what I seem to be. So many people have stretched out their hands and helped me along my wander. With the eye of faith, some have beheld me at Hell's dark door, with no rudder in my hand, and no light in my heart, and steered me to a peace within. Some others have flown into that awful place west and south of old original Hell and, with great compassion, lifted me off of the blistering coals and showed me trees and flowers. All these are the powers and privileges of friendship.

So many evidences of friendship have been revealed to me, that time and paper would not bear the load. Friendships of a moment, an hour or a day, that were nevertheless important, by humble folk whose names have become dusted over, while the feeling of the touch remained, friendly expression having ways like musk. It can throw light back on a day that was so dark, that even the sun refused to take responsibility for it.

It was decreed in the beginning of things that I should meet Mrs. R. Osgood Mason. She had been in the last of my prophetic visions from the first coming of them. I could not know that until I met her. But the moment I walked into the room, I knew that this was the end. There were the two women just as I had always seen them, but always in my dream the faces were misty. Miss Cornelia Chapin was arranging a huge bowl of Calla lilies as I entered the room. There were the strange flowers I had always seen. Her posture was as I had seen it hundreds of times. Mrs. Mason was seated in a chair and everything about her was as I knew it. Only now I could see her face. Born so widely apart in every way, the key to certain phases of my life had been placed in her hand. I had been sent to her to get it. I owe her and owe her and owe her! Not only for material help, but for spiritual guidance.

With the exception of Godmother, Carl Van Vechten has bawled me out more times than anyone else I know. He has not been one of those white "friends of the Negro" who seeks to earn it cheaply by being eternally complimentary. If he is

268

your friend, he will point out your failings as well as your good points in the most direct manner. Take it or leave it. If you can't stand him that way, you need not bother. If he is not interested in you one way or another, he will tell you that, too, in the most off-hand manner, but he is as true as the equator if he is for you. I offer him and his wife Fania Marinoff my humble and sincere thanks.

Both as her secretary and as a friend, Fanny Hurst has picked on me to my profit. She is a curious mixture of little girl and very sophisticated woman. You have to stop and look at her closely to tell which she is from moment to moment. Her transitions are quick as lightning and just as mysterious. I have watched her under all kinds of conditions, and she never ceases to amaze me. Behold her phoning to a swanky hotel for reservations for herself and the Princess Zora, *and* parading me in there all dressed up as an Asiatic person of royal blood and keeping a straight face while the attendants goggled at me and bowed low! Like a little girl, I have known her in the joy of a compelling new gown to take me to tea in some exclusive spot in New York. I would be the press agent for her dress, for everybody was sure to look if *they* saw somebody like me strolling into the Astor or the Biltmore. She can wear clothes and who knows it is her? On the spur of the moment she has taken me galloping over thousands of miles of this North American continent in my Chevrolet for a lark, and then just as suddenly decided to return and go to work. In one moment after figuratively playing with her dolls, she is deep in some social problem. She has been my good friend for many years, and I love her.

To the James Huberts, of Urban League fame, I offer something precious from the best of my treasures. If ever I came to feel that they no longer cared, I would be truly miserable. They elected me to be a Hubert and I mean to hold them to it.

To the Beers, Eleanor Beer de Chetelat, and her mother, Mrs. George W. Beer, twenty-one guns!

I am indebted to Amy Spingarn in a most profound manner. She knows what I mean by that.

Harry T. Burleigh, composer of "Deep River" and other great tunes, worked on me while I was a student to give me perspective and poise. He kept on saying that Negroes did not aim high enough as a rule. They mistook talent for art. One must work. Art was more than inspiration. Besides, he used to take me out to eat in good places to get me used to things. He looks like Otto Kahn in brownskin *and* behaves like a maharajah, with which I do not quarrel.

Of the people who have served me, Bob Wunsch is a man who has no superiors and few equals. Where the man gets all of his soul meat from, I really would like to know. All the greed and grime of the world passes him and never touches him, somehow. I wish that I could make him into a powder and season up the human dough so something could be made out of it. He has enough flavoring in him to do it.

The way I can say how I feel about Dr. Henry Allen Moe is to say that he is twin brother to Bob Wunsch. You cannot talk to the man without feeling that you could have done better in the past and rushing out to improve up from where you are. He has something glinty inside of him that he can't hide. If you have seen him, you have been helped.

I have said that I am grateful to the Charles S. Johnsons and I mean it. Not one iota of their kindness to me has been forgotten.

I fell in love with Jane Belo because she is not what she is supposed to be. She has brains and talent and uses them when she was born rich and pretty, and could have gotten along without any sense. She spent years in Bali studying native custom. She returned to America and went down into the deep South to make comparative studies, with me along. Often as we rode down lonesome roads in South Carolina, I wondered about her tremendous mental energy, and my admiration grew and grew. I also wondered at times why she liked me so much. Certainly it was not from want of friends. Being born of a rich Texas family, familiar with the drawing rooms of America and the continent, she certainly is not starved for company. Yet she thinks that I am a desirable friend to have, and acts like it. Now, she is married to Dr. Frank Tannenbaum, Department of History, Columbia University, and they have a farm up the state and actually milk cows. She draws and paints well enough to make a living at it if she had to, has written things in Anthropology that Dr. Margaret Mead approves of, milks cows and sets her little hat over her nose. How can you place a person like that? I give up. She can just keep on being my friend, and I'll let somebody else explain her.

I value Miguel and Rose Covarrubias for old time's sake. Long before they were married, we polished off many a fried chicken together. Along with Harry Block, we fried "hand chicken" (jointed fried chicken to be eaten with the hand) and settled the affairs of the world over the bones. We did many amusing but senseless things, and kept up our brain power by eating more chicken. Maybe that is why Miguel is such a fine artist. He has hewed to the line, and never let his success induce him to take to trashy foods on fancy plates.

James Weldon Johnson and his wife Grace did much to make my early years in New York pleasant and profitable. I have never seen any other two people who could be right so often, and charming about it at the same time.

Walter White and his glamorous Gladys used to have me over and feed me on good fried chicken in my student days for no other reason than that they just wanted to. They have lent me some pleasant hours. I mean to pay them back sometime.

There are so many others, Colonel and Mrs. Bert Lippincott, Frank Frazier, Paul and Eslanda Robeson, Lawrence Brown, Calvin J. Ferguson, Dr. Edwin Osgood Grover, Dr. Hamilton Holt, H. P. Davis, J. P. McEvoy, Edna St. Vincent Millay, Dr. and Mrs. Simeon L. Carson of Washington, D.C., along with Betram Barker. As I said in the beginning of this, that I was a precious gift, what there is of me. I could not find space for all of the donors on paper, though there is plenty of room in my heart. I am just sort of assembled up together out of friendship and put together by time.

Josephine Van Doltzen Pease, that sprout of an old Philadelphia family who writes such charming stories for children, and our mutual friend, Edith Darling Thompson, are right inside the most inside part of my heart. They are both sacred figures on my altar when I deck it to offer something to love.

How could I ever think I could make out without that remarkable couple Whit Burnett and Martha Foley? I just happened to put his name down first. Either way you take that family, it's got a head to it. One head with whiskers to it, and one plain, but both real heads. Even little David, their son, has got his mind made up. Being little, he gets over-ruled at times, but he knows what he wants to do and puts a lot of vim into the thing. It is not his fault if Whit and Martha have ideas of censorship. I have no idea what he will pick out to do by the time he gets grown, but, whatever it is, you won't find any bewildered David Foley-Burnett wandering around. I'll bet you a fat man on that. Two fat men to your skinny one.

Another California crowd that got me liking them and grateful too, is that Herbert Childs, with his cherub-looking wife.

Katharane Edson Mershon has been a good friend to me. She is a person of immense understanding. It makes me sit and ponder. I do not know whether her ready sympathy grows out of her own experiences, or whether it was always there and only expanded by having struggled herself. I suppose it is both.

She was born of Katherine Philips Edson, the woman who put the minimum wage law for women on the statute books of California. It was no fault of hers that dirty politics later rubbed it out. She did many other things for the good of California, like fighting for the preservation of the Redwood forests. She sat, a lone woman, in the Washington Disarmament Conference, and, after forty, sent her two sons through good colleges by the sweat of her brow.

So Katharane Edson Mershon probably inherited some feelings. Anyway, she took life in her hands and hied herself away from home at sixteen and went forth to dance for inside expression. She did important things in the now famous Play House of Pasadena, conducted a school of dance and was a director for the famous school of Ruth St. Denis. After she married, she spent nine years in Bali, conducting a clinic at her own expense. More than that, she did not do it by proxy. She was there every day, giving medicine for fever, washing sores and sitting by the dying. Dancing was her way of doing things but she was impelled by mercy into this other field. Her husband was with her in this. His main passion is making gardens, but he threw himself into the clinic with enthusiasm.

For me, she gave me back my health and my hope, and I have her to thank for the sparing of my unprofitable life.

Jack Mershon, husband of Katharane's heart, is the son of William B. Mershon of Saginaw, Michigan. This William B. went into the Michigan forests and hacked him out a fortune. Tough as whit leather, with a passion for hunting and fishing, he nevertheless is one of the best informed men in the world on Americana, with especial emphasis on the Northwest. He has endowed parks, settlements, replanted whole forests of millions of trees in Michigan, and done things to make Saginaw a fine city, which the younger generation knows little about, because he himself says nothing.

Jack like his wife ran off from home and supported himself on the stage. He is soft in manner, but now and then you can see some of the gruff old stuff of William B. Mershon oozing through his hide. That same kind of mule-headedness on one side and generosity on the other. He will probably never be a hard-cussing, hard-driving empire builder like his old man, but what he aims to do, he does.

Mrs. Mershon invited me out to California, and a story starts from that. Being trustful and full of faith, I hurried out there. She fed me well, called in the doctors and cleared the malaria out of my marrow, took me to I. Magnin's and dressed me up. I was just burning up with gratitude and still did not suspect a thing.

Then I began to notice a leer in her eye! This woman had designs on me. I could tell that from her look, but I could not tell what it was. I should have known! I should have been suspicious, but I was dumb to the fact and did not suspect a thing until I was ambushed.

One day she said to me off-hand, "You ought to see a bit of California while you are out here."

"Oh, that would be fine!" I crackled and gleamed at the idea. So I saw California! At first, I thought it was just to give *me* some pleasure, but I soon found out it was the gleeful malice of a Californiac taking revenge upon a poor defenseless Florida Fiend.

She fried me in the deserts, looking at poppies, succulents (cactus, to you and everybody else except Californiacs), Joshua trees, kiln dried lizards and lupin bushes. Just look at those wild lilacs! Observe that chaparrel! Don't miss that juniper. Don't say you haven't seen our cottonwood. Regard those nobles (California oaks).

Next thing I know, we would be loping up some rough-back mountain and every hump and hollow would be pointed out to me. No need for me to murmur that I had to watch the road while driving. Just look at that peak! Now! You can look down over that rim. When I took refuge in watching the road, she switched technique on me. Her husband, Jack Mershon, was pressed into service, so all I had to do was to sit in the back seat of the Buick while Katharane twisted my head from side to side and pointed out the sights.

From San Diego up, we looked at every wave on the Pacific, lizards, bushes, prune and orange groves, date palms, eucalyptus, gullies with and without water that these Californiacs call rivers, asphalt pits where the remains of prehistoric animals had been found, the prehistoric bones in person, saber-tooth tigers, short-faced bears (bears, before bears saw Californiacs and pulled long faces), old fashioned elephants that ran mostly to teeth, saurians and what not. Then there was barracuda and shark meat, abalones, beaches full of people in dark sun glasses, Hollywood, and slacks with hips in them all swearing

274

to God and other responsible characters that they sure look pretty, and most of them lying and unrepentant. Man! I saw Southern California, and thought I had done something. Me, being from Florida, I had held my peace, and only murmured now and then a hint or two about our own climate and trees and things like that. Nothing offensive, you understand. I wouldn't really say how good it was, because I wanted to be polite. So I drew a long breath when we had prospected over Southern California, and I had kept from exploding.

"Now, I shall take you to see Northern California—the best part of the state," my fiendish friend gloated. "Ah, the mountains!"

"But, I don't care too much about mountains," I murmured through the alkali in my mouth.

"You are going to see it just the same. You are not going back east and pretend you saw none of the beauty of my state. You are going to see California, and like it—you Florida Fiend. Just because your Florida mud-turtles have been used to bogging down in swamps and those Everglades, whatever they are—and they don't sound like much to me, is no reason for you to ignore the beauties of California mountains. Let's go!"

So we went north. We drove over rocky ridges and stopped on ledges miles up in the air and gazed upon the Pacific. Redwood forests, Golden Gates, cable cars, missions, gaps, gullies, San Simeon-with-William Randolph Hearst, Monterey-with-history, Carmel-with-artists and atmosphere, Big Sur and Santa Barbara, Bay Bridges and Giant Sequoia, Alcatraz, wharves, Capitol buildings, mountains that didn't have sense enough to know it was summer and time to take off their winter clothes, seals, sealrocks, and then seals on seal-rocks, pelicans and pelican rocks and then that [ ] Pacific!

Finally, back at Carmel, I struck. A person has just so many places to bump falling down rocky cliffs. But did I escape? No, indeed! I was standing on a big pile of bony rocks on Point Lobos, when I announced that I thought I (sort of) had the idea of California and knew what it was about.

"Oh, no!" Katharane grated maliciously. "Seen California! Why, this is the second largest state in the Union! You haven't half seen it, but you are going to. I've got you out here and I mean to rub your nose in California. You are going to see it, I'm here to tell you." So on we went. I saw, and I saw and I *saw*! Man! I tell you that I saw California. For instance, I saw the hats in San Francisco! Finally, I came to the conclusion that in Los Angeles the women get hats imposed upon them. In San Francisco, they go out in the woods and shoot 'em.

Then after I had galloped from one end of the state to the other and from edge to ocean and back again, Katharane Mershon up and tells me, "All I wanted you to see was the redwoods!"

I mean to write to the Florida Chamber of Commerce and get them to trick a gang of Californiacs to Florida and let me be the guide. It is going to be good, and I wouldn't fool you. From Key West to the Perdido river they are going to see every orange tree, rattlesnake, gopher, coudar, palm tree, sand pile, beach mango tree, sapodilla, kumquat, alligator, tourist trap, celery patch, bean field, strawberry, lake, jook, gulf, ocean and river in between, and if their constitutions sort of wear away, it will be unfortunate, but one of the hazards of war.

But California is nice. *Buen* nice! Of course they lie about the California climate a little more than we do about ours, but you don't hold that against them. They have to, to rank up with us. But at that this California is a swell state, especially from Santa Barbara on north. Of course, coming from Florida, I feel like the man when he saw a hunch back for the first time—it seems that California does wear its hips a bit high. I mean all those mountains. Too much of the state is standing up on edge. To my notion, land is supposed to lie down and be walked on—not rearing up, staring you in the face. It is too biggity and imposing. But on the whole, California will do for a lovely state until God can make up something better. So I forgive Katharane Mershon for showing me the place. Another score for friendship.

276

Therefore, I can say that I have had friends. Friendship is a mysterious and ocean-bottom thing. Who can know the outer ranges of it? Perhaps no human being has ever explored its limits. Anyway, God must have thought well of it when He made it. Make the attempt if you want to, but you will find that trying to go through life without friendship, is like milking a bear to get cream for your morning coffee. It is a whole lot of trouble, and then not worth much after you get it.

11:00 A.M. July 20, 1941
1392 Hull Lane
Altadena, California

CONCERT

And now, I must mention something, not because it means so much to me, but because it did mean something to others.

On January 10, 1932, I presented a Negro Folk Concert at the John Golden Theater in New York.

I am not a singer, a dancer, nor even a musician. I was, therefore, seeking no reputation in either field. I did the concert because I knew that nowhere had the general public ever heard Negro music as done by Negroes. There had been numerous concerts of Negro spirituals by famous Negro singers, but none as it was done by, let us say, Macedonia Baptist Church. They had been tampered with by musicians, and had their faces lifted to the degree that when real Negroes heard them, they sat back and listened just like white audiences did. It was just as strange to them as to the Swedes, for example. Beautiful songs and arrangements but going under the wrong titles.

Here was the difference. When I was coming up, I had heard songs and singing. People made the tunes and sang them because they were pretty and satisfied something. Then I got away from home and learned about "holler singing." Holler singing or classic, if you want to call it that, is not done for the sake of agreeable sound. It is a sporting proposition. The singer, after years of training, puts out a brag that he or she can perform certain tricks with the voice, and the audience comes and bets him the admission price that he can't do it. They lean back in the seats and wait eagerly for the shake, the high jump or the low dive. If the performer makes it, he rakes in the pot. If not, he can go back and yell "Whoa! Har! Gee!" to some mule.

I saw that Negro music and musicians were getting lost in the betting ring. I did not hope to stop the ones who were ambitious to qualify as holler experts. That was all right in its place. I just wanted people to know what real Negro music sounded like. There were the two things.

Of course, I had known this all along, but my years of research accented this situation inside of me and troubled me. Was the real voice of my people never to be heard? This ersatz Negro music was getting on. It was like the story from Hans Christian Andersen where the shadow became the man. That would not have been important if the arrangements had been better music than the originals, but they were not. They conformed more to Conservatory rules of music but that is not saying much. They were highly flavored with Bach and Brahms, and Gregorian chants, but why drag them in? It seemed to me a determined effort to squeeze all of the rich black juice out of the songs and present a sort of musical octoroon to the public. Like some more "passing for white."

Now in collecting tales and hoodoo rituals, I had taken time out to collect a mass of Negro songs of all descriptions. I was not supposed to do that, but I could not resist it. Sitting around in saw-mill quarters, turpentine camps, prison camps, railroad camps and jooks, I soaked them in as I went. My people are not going to do but so much of anything before they sing something. I always encouraged it because I loved it and could not be different. I brought this mass home, seeing all the possibilities for some Negro musicians to do something fine with it.

Being a friend of Hall Johnson's, I turned it over to him to use as he wished with his concert group. He kept it for nearly a year. I called him up about it two or three times and finally he told me that he saw no use for it. The public only wanted to hear spirituals, and spirituals that had been well arranged. I knew that he was mistaken, for white people used to crowd Zion Hope Baptist Church, where my father was pastor to hear the singing, and there certainly were no trained musicians around there. I had seen it in various Negro churches where the congregations just grabbed hold of a tune and everybody worked on it in his or her own way to magnificent harmonic effect. I knew that they liked the work songs, for I had seen them park their cars by a gang of workers just to listen to what happened. So in spite of what he said, I kept to my own convictions.

When he gave me back the songs, I talked about a real Negro concert for a while, to anybody who would listen, and then decided to do it. But I felt that I did not know enough to do it alone.

Not only did I want the singing very natural, I wanted to display West Indian folk dancing. I had been out in the Bahama Islands collecting material and had witnessed the dynamic Fire Dance which had three parts; the Jumping Dance, The Ring Play and the Congo. It was so stirring and magnificent that I had to admit to myself that we had nothing in America to equal it. I went to the dancing every chance I got, and took pains to learn them. I could just see an American audience being thrilled.

So the first step I took was to assemble a troup of sixteen Bahamans who could dance. Then I went back to Hall Johnson with the proposition that we combine his singers and my dancers for a dramatic concert. I had the script all written. It was a dramatization of a working day on a Florida railroad camp with the Fire Dance for a climax. Hall Johnson looked it over and agreed to the thing.

But his mind must have changed, because I took my dancers up to his studio four times, but the rehearsals never came off. Twice he was not even there. Once he said he had a rehearsal of his own group which could not be put off, and once there was no explanation. Besides, something unfortunate happened. While my dancers sat around me and waited, two or three of the singers talked in stage whispers about "monkey chasers dancing." They ridiculed the whole idea. Who wanted to be mixed up with anything like that?

The American Negroes have the unfortunate habit of speaking of West Indians as "monkey-chasers," pretending to believe that the West Indians catch monkeys and stew them with rice.

I heard what was being said very distinctly, but I hoped that my group did not. But they did and began to show hurt in their faces. I could not let them feel that I shared the foolish prejudice, which I do not, so I had to make a move. I showed my resentment, gathered my folks, and we all went down to my place in 66th Street. It looked as if I were licked. I had spoken to a man in Judson's Bureau in Steinway Hall about booking us, and now it all looked hopeless. So I went down next day to call it all off.

He said I ought to go ahead. It sounded fine to him. But go ahead on my own. He happened to know that Gaston, Hall Johnson's manager, wanted me headed off. He saw in my idea a threat to Hall Johnson's group. "You are being strung along on this rehearsal gag to throw you off. Go ahead on your own."

So I went ahead. We rehearsed at my house, here and there, and anywhere. The secretary to John Golden liked the idea after seeing a rehearsal and got me the theater. She undertook to handle the press for me, so I just turned over the money to her and she did well by me.

I had talked Godmother, Mrs. R. Osgood Mason, into helping me. Dr. Locke, her main Negro confidant, had opposed it at first, but he was finally won over. You see, he had been born in Philadelphia, educated at Harvard and Oxford and had never known the common run of Negroes. He was not at all sympathetic to our expression. To his credit, he has changed his viewpoint.

Then came that Sunday night of the tenth. We had a good house, mostly white shirt fronts and ermine. Godmother was out there sitting close enough for me to see her and encourage me. Locke was there, too, in faultless tails. He came back stage to give me a pat of encouragement and went back out front. I needed it. I was as nervous as I could be, and if I had known then as much as I know now, I would have been even more nervous. Fools rush in where angels fear to tread.

From the lifting of the curtain on the dawn scene where the shack rouser awakens the camp to the end of the first half, it was evident that the audience was with us. The male chorus "lined track" and "spiked" to tremendous applause. The curtain had to be lifted and lowered and then again. I was standing there in the wings still shivering, when Lee Whipper, who had played the part of the itinerant preacher in a beautiful manner, gave me a shove and I found myself out on the stage. A tremendous burst of applause met me, and so I had to say something.

I explained why I had done it. That music without motion was unnatural with Negroes, and what I had tried to do was to present Negro singing in a natural way—with action. I don't know what else I said, but the audience was kind and I walked off to an applauding house.

Right here, let me set something straight. Godmother had meant for me to call Dr. Locke to the stage to make any explanations, but she had not told me. Neither had Locke told me. I was stupid. When he told me where he would be sitting, he evidently thought that would be enough. But I had not thought of any speech in all my troubles of rehearsals, making costumes and keeping things going. It just had not occurred to me. I would not have been out there myself if Lee Whipper had not shoved me. I found out later that I had seemed to ignore Dr. Locke, for which I am very sorry. I would have much rather had him make a thought-out speech than my improvising. It just did not occur to me in all my excitement. It may be too late, but I ask him please to pardon me. He had been helpful and I meant him good.

The second half of the program went off even better than the first. As soon as the curtain went up on the Fire Dancers, their costuming got a hand. It broke out time and again during the dancing and thundered as Caroline Rich and Strawn executed the last movement with the group as a back-ground. It was good it was the last thing, for nothing could have followed it.

Hall Johnson did a generous thing. I had sent tickets and he and his manager came back stage and Hall said, "You proved your point all right. When you talked to me about it, it sounded like a crazy mess. I really came to see you do a flop, but it was swell!" I thought that was fine of Hall.

The New School of Social Research presented us six weeks later and we danced at the Vanderbilt, Nyack, and various places. But I was worn out with back stage arguments, eternal demands for money, a disturbance in my dance group because one of the men, who was incidentally the poorest dancer of all, preached that I was an American exploiting them and they ought to go ahead under his guidance. Stew-Beef, Lias Strawn and Motor-Boat pointed out to him that they had never dreamed of dancing in public until I had picked them up. I had rehearsed them for months, fed them and routined them into something. Why had *he* never thought of it before I did. He had discouraged the others from joining me until it began to look successful. So they meant to stick with me, American or no American. But two of the women joined the trouble maker and I fired all three of them. The whole thing was beginning to wear me down. When some other things began to annoy me, I decided to go home to Florida and try to write the book I had in mind, which was *Jonah's Gourd Vine*. Before it was hardly started, I heard that Hall Johnson had raided my group and was using it in his "Run Little Chillun." I never saw the production, but I was told that the religious scene was the spitting image of the one from my concert also. As I said, I never saw it so I wouldn't know.

But this I do know, that people became very much alive to West Indian dancing and work songs. I have heard myself over the air dozens of times and felt the influence of that concert running through what has been done since. My name is never mentioned, of course, because that is not the way theater people do things, but that concert and the rave notices I got from the critics shoved the viewpoint over towards the natural Negro.

Theater Arts Magazine photographed us and presented us in its April issue following the concert at the John Golden. The Folk Dance Society presented us at the Vanderbilt. We appeared at the first National Folk Festival in St. Louis in 1934, at Chicago in 1934, and at Constitution Hall in Washington, D.C. In Chicago, I had only ten days to try to prepare a full length program and it was not smooth considering that I had only very raw material to work with in so short a time, but at that the dancers and a dramatic bit went over splendidly and got good notices. Katherine Dunham loaned us her studio for rehearsal twice, which was kind of her. Anyway, West Indian dancing had gone west and created interest just as it had done in the east. When I got to Jamaica on my first Guggenheim fellowship in 1936, I found that Katherine Dunham had been there a few months before collecting dances, and had gone on to Haiti.

I made no real money out of my concert work. I might have done so if I had taken it up as a life work. But I am satisfied in knowing that I established a trend and pointed Negro expression back towards the saner ground of our own unbelievable originality.

AFTERWORD

❖

ZORA NEALE HURSTON:
"A NEGRO WAY OF SAYING"

I.

The Reverend Harry Middleton Hyatt, an Episcopal priest whose five-volume classic collection, *Hoodoo, Conjuration, Witchcraft, and Rootwork,* more than amply returned an investment of forty years' research, once asked me during an interview in 1977 what had become of another eccentric collector whom he admired. "I met her in the field in the thirties. I think," he reflected for a few seconds, "that her first name was Zora." It was an innocent question, made reasonable by the body of confused and often contradictory rumors that make Zora Neale Hurston's own legend as richly curious and as dense as are the black myths she did so much to preserve in her classic anthropological works, *Mules and Men* and *Tell My Horse,* and in her fiction.

A graduate of Barnard, where she studied under Franz Boas, Zora Neale Hurston published seven books—four novels, two books of folklore, and an autobiography—and more than fifty shorter works between the middle of the Harlem Renaissance and the end of the Korean War, when she was the dominant black woman writer in the United States. The dark obscurity into which her career then lapsed reflects her staunchly independent political stances rather than any deficiency of craft or vision. Virtually ignored after the early fifties, even by the Black Arts movement in the sixties, an otherwise noisy and intense spell of black image- and myth-making that rescued so many black writers from remaindered oblivion, Hurston embodied a more or less harmonious but nevertheless problematic unity of opposites. It is this complexity that refuses to lend itself to the glib categories of "radical" or "conservative," "black" or "Negro," "revolutionary" or "Uncle Tom"—categories of little use in literary criticism. It is this same complexity, embodied in her fiction, that, until Alice Walker published her important essay ("In Search of Zora Neale Hurston") in *Ms.* magazine in 1975, had made Hurston's place in black literary history an ambiguous one at best.

The rediscovery of Afro-American writers has usually turned on larger political criteria, of which the writer's work is supposedly a mere reflection. The deeply satisfying aspect of the rediscovery of Zora Neale Hurston is that black women generated it primarily to establish a maternal literary ancestry. Alice Walker's moving essay recounts her attempts to find Hurston's unmarked grave in the Garden of the Heavenly Rest, a segregated cemetery in Fort Pierce, Florida. Hurston became a metaphor for the black woman writer's search for tradition. The craft of Alice Walker, Gayl Jones, Gloria Naylor, and Toni Cade Bambara bears, in markedly different ways, strong affinities with Hurston's. Their attention to Hurston signifies a novel sophistication in black literature: they read Hurston not only for the spiritual kinship inherent in such relations but because she used black vernacular speech and rituals, in ways subtle and various, to chart the coming to consciousness of black women, so glaringly absent in other black fiction. This use of the vernacular became the fundamental framework for all but one of her novels and is particularly effective in her classic work *Their Eyes Were Watching God,*

288

published in 1937, which is more closely related to Henry James's *The Portrait of a Lady* and Jean Toomer's *Cane* than to Langston Hughes's and Richard Wright's proletarian literature, so popular in the Depression.

The charting of Janie Crawford's fulfillment as an autonomous imagination, *Their Eyes* is a lyrical novel that correlates the need of her first two husbands for ownership of progressively larger physical space (and the gaudy accoutrements of upward mobility) with the suppression of self-awareness in their wife. Only with her third and last lover, a roustabout called Tea Cake whose unstructured frolics center around and about the Florida swamps, does Janie at last bloom, as does the large pear tree that stands beside her grandmother's tiny log cabin.

> She saw a dust bearing bee sink into the sanctum of a bloom; the thousand sister calyxes arch to meet the love embrace and the ecstatic shiver of the tree from root to tiniest branch creaming in every blossom and frothing with delight. So this was a marriage!

To plot Janie's journey from object to subject, the narrative of the novel shifts from third to a blend of first and third person (known as "free indirect discourse"), signifying this awareness of self in Janie. *Their Eyes* is a bold feminist novel, the first to be explicitly so in the Afro-American tradition. Yet in its concern with the project of finding a voice, with language as an instrument of injury and salvation, of selfhood and empowerment, it suggests many of the themes that inspirit Hurston's oeuvre as a whole.

II.

One of the most moving passages in American literature is Zora Neale Hurston's account of her last encounter with her dying mother, found in a chapter entitled "Wandering" in her autobiography, *Dust Tracks on a Road* (1942):

As I crowded in, they lifted up the bed and turned it around so that Mama's eyes would face east. I thought that she looked to me as the head of the bed reversed. Her mouth was slightly open, but her breathing took up so much of her strength that she could not talk. But she looked at me, or so I felt, to speak for her. She depended on me for a voice.

We can begin to understand the rhetorical distance that separated Hurston from her contemporaries if we compare this passage with a similar scene published just three years later in *Black Boy* by Richard Wright, Hurston's dominant black male contemporary and rival: "Once, in the night, my mother called me to her bed and told me that she could not endure the pain, and she wanted to die. I held her hand and begged her to be quiet. That night I ceased to react to my mother; my feelings were frozen." If Hurston represents her final moments with her mother in terms of the search for voice, then Wright attributes to a similar experience a certain "somberness of spirit that I was never to lose," which "grew into a symbol in my mind, gathering to itself . . . the poverty, the ignorance, the helplessness. . . ." Few authors in the black tradition have less in common than Zora Neale Hurston and Richard Wright. And whereas Wright would reign through the forties as our predominant author, Hurston's fame reached its zenith in 1943 with a *Saturday Review* cover story honoring the success of *Dust Tracks.* Seven years later, she would be serving as a maid in Rivo Alto, Florida; ten years after that she would die in the County Welfare Home in Fort Pierce, Florida.

How could the recipient of two Guggenheims and the author of four novels, a dozen short stories, two musicals, two books on black mythology, dozens of essays, and a prizewinning autobiography virtually "disappear" from her readership for three full decades? There are no easy answers to this quandary, despite the concerted attempts of scholars to resolve it. It is clear, however, that the loving, diverse, and

290

enthusiastic responses that Hurston's work engenders today were not shared by several of her influential black male contemporaries. The reasons for this are complex and stem largely from what we might think of as their "racial ideologies."

Part of Hurston's received heritage—and perhaps the paramount received notion that links the novel of manners in the Harlem Renaissance, the social realism of the thirties, and the cultural nationalism of the Black Arts movement—was the idea that racism had reduced black people to mere ciphers, to beings who only react to an omnipresent racial oppression, whose culture is "deprived" where different, and whose psyches are in the main "pathological." Albert Murray, the writer and social critic, calls this "the Social Science Fiction Monster." Socialists, separatists, and civil rights advocates alike have been devoured by this beast.

Hurston thought this idea degrading, its propagation a trap, and railed against it. It was, she said, upheld by "the sobbing school of Negrohood who hold that nature somehow has given them a dirty deal." Unlike Hughes and Wright, Hurston chose deliberately to ignore this "false picture that distorted. . . ." Freedom, she wrote in *Moses, Man of the Mountain,* "was something internal. . . . The man himself must make his own emancipation." And she declared her first novel a manifesto against the "arrogance" of whites assuming that "black lives are only defensive reactions to white actions." Her strategy was not calculated to please.

What we might think of as Hurston's mythic realism, lush and dense within a lyrical black idiom, seemed politically retrograde to the proponents of a social or critical realism. If Wright, Ellison, Brown, and Hurston were engaged in a battle over ideal fictional modes with which to represent the Negro, clearly Hurston lost the battle.

But not the war.

After Hurston and her choice of style for the black novel were silenced for nearly three decades, what we have witnessed since is clearly a marvelous instance of the return of the repressed. For Zora Neale Hurston has been "rediscovered" in a manner unprecedented in the black tradition: several black women writers, among whom are some of the most accomplished writers in America today, have openly turned to her works as sources of narrative strategies, to be repeated, imitated, and revised, in acts of textual bonding. Responding to Wright's critique, Hurston claimed that she had wanted at long last to write a black novel, and "not a treatise on sociology." It is this urge that resonates in Toni Morrison's *Song of Solomon* and *Beloved,* and in Walker's depiction of Hurston as our prime symbol of "racial health—a sense of black people as complete, complex, *undiminished* human beings, a sense that is lacking in so much black writing and literature." In a tradition in which male authors have ardently denied black literary paternity, this is a major development, one that heralds the refinement of our notion of tradition: Zora and her daughters are a tradition-within-the-tradition, a black woman's voice.

The resurgence of popular and academic readerships of Hurston's works signifies her multiple canonization in the black, the American, and the feminist traditions. Within the critical establishment, scholars of every stripe have found in Hurston texts for all seasons. More people have read Hurston's works since 1975 than did between that date and the publication of her first novel, in 1934.

III.

Rereading Hurston, I am always struck by the density of intimate experiences she cloaked in richly elaborated imagery. It is this concern for the figurative capacity of black language, for what a character in *Mules and Men* calls "a hidden meaning, jus' like de Bible . . . de inside meanin' of words," that unites Hurston's anthropological studies with her fiction. For the folklore Hurston collected so meticulously as Franz Boas's student at Barnard became metaphors, allegories, and performances in her novels, the traditional recurring canonical metaphors of black culture. Always more of a novelist than a social scientist, even Hurston's academic collections center on the quality of imagination that makes these lives whole and splendid. But it is in the novel that Hurston's use of the black idiom realizes its fullest effect. In *Jonah's Gourd Vine,* her first novel, for instance, the errant preacher, John, as described by Robert Hemenway "is a poet who graces his world with language but cannot find the words to secure his own personal grace." This concern for language and for the "natural" poets who "bring barbaric splendor of word and song into the very camp of the mockers" not only connects her two disciplines but also makes of "the suspended linguistic moment" a thing to behold indeed. Invariably, Hurston's writing depends for its strength on the text, not the context, as does John's climactic sermon, a *tour de force* of black image and metaphor. Image and metaphor define John's world; his failure to interpret himself leads finally to his self-destruction. As Robert Hemenway, Hurston's biographer, concludes, "Such passages eventually add up to a theory of language and behavior."

Using "the spy-glass of Anthropology," her work celebrates rather than moralizes; it shows rather than tells, such that "both behavior and art become self-evident as the tale texts and hoodoo rituals accrete during the reading." As author, she functions as "a midwife participating in the birth of a body of folklore, . . . the first wondering contacts with natural law." The myths she describes so accurately are in fact "alternative modes for perceiving reality," and never just condescending depictions of the quaint. Hurston sees "the Dozens," for example, that age-old black ritual of graceful insult, as, among other things, a verbal defense of the sanctity of the family, conjured through ingenious plays on words. Though attacked by Wright and virtually ignored by his literary heirs, Hurston's ideas about language and craft undergird many of the most successful contributions to Afro-American literature that followed.

IV.

We can understand Hurston's complex and contradictory legacy more fully if we examine *Dust Tracks on a Road,* her own controversial account of her life. Hurston did make significant parts of herself up, like a masquerader putting on a disguise for the ball, like a character in her fictions. In this way, Hurston *wrote* herself, and sought in her works to rewrite the "self" of "the race," in its several private and public guises, largely for ideological reasons. That which she chooses to reveal is the life of her imagination, as it sought to mold and interpret her environment. That which she silences or deletes, similarly, is all that her readership would draw upon to delimit or pigeonhole her life as a synecdoche of "the race problem," an exceptional part standing for the debased whole.

Hurston's achievement in *Dust Tracks* is twofold. First, she gives us a *writer's* life, rather than an account, as she says, of "the Negro problem." So many events in this text are figured in terms of Hurston's growing awareness and mastery of books and language, language and linguistic rituals as spoken and written both by masters of the Western tradition and by ordinary members of the black community. These two "speech communities," as it were, are Hurston's great sources of inspiration not only in her novels but also in her autobiography.

The representation of her sources of language seems to be her principal concern, as she constantly shifts back and forth between her "literate" narrator's voice and a highly idiomatic black voice found in wonderful passages of free indirect discourse. Hurston moves in and out of these distinct voices effortlessly, seamlessly, just as she does in *Their Eyes* to chart Janie's coming to consciousness. It is this usage of a *divided* voice, a double voice unreconciled, that strikes me as her great achievement, a verbal analogue of her double experiences as a woman in a male-dominated world and as a black person in a nonblack world, a woman writer's revision of W. E. B.

Du Bois's metaphor of "double-consciousness" for the hyphenated African-American.

Her language, variegated by the twin voices that intertwine throughout the text, retains the power to unsettle.

There is something about poverty that smells like death.
Dead dreams dropping off the heart like leaves in a dry
season and rotting around the feet; impulses smothered too
long in the fetid air of underground caves. The soul lives
in a sickly air. People can be slave-ships in shoes.

Elsewhere she analyzes black "idioms" used by a culture "raised on simile and invective. They know how to call names," she concludes, then lists some, such as 'gator-mouthed, box-ankled, puzzle-gutted, shovel-footed: "Eyes looking like skint-ginny nuts, and mouth looking like a dish-pan full of broke-up crockery!"

Immediately following the passage about her mother's death, she writes:

The Master-Maker in His making had made Old Death.
Made him with big, soft feet and square toes. Made him
with a face that reflects the face of all things, but neither
changes itself, nor is mirrored anywhere. Made the body of
death out of infinite hunger. Made a weapon of his hand to
satisfy his needs. This was the morning of the day of the
beginning of things.

Language, in these passages, is not merely "adornment," as Hurston described a key black linguistic practice; rather, manner and meaning are perfectly in tune: she says the thing in the most meaningful manner. Nor is she being "cute," or pandering to a condescending white readership. She is "naming" emotions, as she says, in a language both deeply personal and culturally specific.

The second reason that *Dust Tracks* succeeds as literature arises from the first: Hurston's unresolved tension between her double voices signifies her full understanding of modernism. Hurston uses the two voices in her text to celebrate the psychological fragmentation both of modernity and of the black American. As Barbara Johnson has written, hers is a rhetoric of division, rather than a fiction of psychological or cultural unity. Zora Neale Hurston, the "real" Zora Neale Hurston that we long to locate in this text, dwells in the silence that separates these two voices: she is both, and neither; bilingual, and mute. This strategy helps to explain her attraction to so many contemporary critics and writers, who can turn to her works again and again only to be startled at her remarkable artistry.

But the life that Hurston could write was not the life she could live. In fact, Hurston's life, so much more readily than does the standard sociological rendering, reveals how economic limits determine our choices even more than does violence or love. Put simply, Hurston wrote well when she was comfortable, wrote poorly when she was not. Financial problems—book sales, grants and fellowships too few and too paltry, ignorant editors and a smothering patron—produced the sort of dependence that affects, if not determines, her style, a relation she explored somewhat ironically in "What White Publishers Won't Print." We cannot oversimplify the relation between Hurston's art and her life; nor can we reduce the complexity of her postwar politics, which, rooted in her distaste for the pathological image of blacks, were markedly conservative and Republican.

Nor can we sentimentalize her disastrous final decade, when she found herself working as a maid on the very day the *Saturday Evening Post* published her short story "Conscience of the Court" and often found herself without money, surviving after 1957 on unemployment benefits, substitute teaching, and welfare checks. "In her last days," Hemenway concludes dispassionately, "Zora lived a difficult life—alone, proud, ill, obsessed with a book she could not finish."

The excavation of her buried life helped a new generation read Hurston again. But ultimately we must find Hurston's legacy in her art, where she "ploughed up some literacy and laid by some alphabets." Her importance rests with the legacy of fiction and lore she constructed so cannily. As Hurston herself noted, "Roll your eyes in ecstasy and ape his every move, but until we have placed something upon his street corner that is our own, we are right back where we were when they filed our iron collar off." If, as a friend eulogized, "She didn't come to you empty," then she does not leave black literature empty. If her earlier obscurity and neglect today seem inconceivable, perhaps now, as she wrote of Moses, she has "crossed over."

HENRY LOUIS GATES, JR.

SELECTED BIBLIOGRAPHY

WORKS BY ZORA NEALE HURSTON

Jonah's Gourd Vine. Philadelphia: J. B. Lippincott, 1934.

Mules and Men. Philadelphia: J. B. Lippincott, 1935.

Their Eyes Were Watching God. Philadelphia: J. B. Lippincott, 1937.

Tell My Horse. Philadelphia: J. B. Lippincott, 1938.

Moses, Man of the Mountain. Philadelphia: J. B. Lippincott, 1939.

Dust Tracks on a Road. Philadelphia: J. B. Lippincott, 1942.

Seraph on the Suwanee. New York: Charles Scribner's Sons, 1948.

I Love Myself When I Am Laughing . . . & Then Again When I Am Looking Mean and Impressive: A Zora Neale Hurston Reader. Edited by Alice Walker. Old Westbury, N.Y.: The Feminist Press, 1979.

The Sanctified Church. Edited by Toni Cade Bambara. Berkeley: Turtle Island, 1981.

Spunk: The Selected Short Stories of Zora Neale Hurston. Berkeley: Turtle Island, 1985.

WORKS ABOUT ZORA NEALE HURSTON

Baker, Houston A., Jr. *Blues, Ideology, and Afro-American Literature: A Vernacular Theory,* pp. 15–63. Chicago: University of Chicago Press, 1984.

Bloom, Harold, ed. *Zora Neale Hurston.* New York: Chelsea House, 1986.

————, ed. *Zora Neale Hurston's "Their Eyes Were Watching God."* New York: Chelsea House, 1987.

Byrd, James W. "Zora Neale Hurston: A Novel Folklorist." *Tennessee Folklore Society Bulletin* 21 (1955): 37–41.

Cooke, Michael G. "Solitude: The Beginnings of Self-Realization in Zora Neale Hurston, Richard Wright, and Ralph Ellison." In Michael G. Cooke, *Afro-American Literature in the Twentieth Century,* pp. 71–110. New Haven: Yale University Press, 1984.

Dance, Daryl C. "Zora Neale Hurston." In *American Women Writers: Bibliographical Essays,* edited by Maurice Duke, et al. Westport, Conn.: Greenwood Press, 1983.

Gates, Henry Louis, Jr. "The Speakerly Text." In Henry Louis Gates, Jr., *The Signifying Monkey,* pp. 170–217. New York: Oxford University Press, 1988.

Giles, James R. "The Significance of Time in Zora Neale Hurston's *Their Eyes Were Watching God."* *Negro American Literature Forum* 6 (Summer 1972): 52–53, 60.

Hemenway, Robert E. *Zora Neale Hurston: A Literary Biography.* Chicago: University of Illinois Press, 1977.

Holloway, Karla. *The Character of the Word: The Texts of Zora Neale Hurston.* Westport, Conn.: Greenwood Press, 1987.

Holt, Elvin. "Zora Neale Hurston." In *Fifty Southern Writers After 1900,* edited by Joseph M. Flura and Robert Bain, pp. 259–69. Westport, Conn.: Greenwood Press, 1987.

Howard, Lillie Pearl. *Zora Neale Hurston.* Boston: Twayne, 1980.

————. "Zora Neale Hurston." In *Dictionary of Literary Biography,* vol. 51, edited by Trudier Harris, pp. 133–45. Detroit: Gale, 1987.

Jackson, Blyden. "Some Negroes in the Land of Goshen." *Tennessee Folklore Society Bulletin* 19 (4) (December 1953): 103–7.

Johnson, Barbara. "Metaphor, Metonymy, and Voice in *Their Eyes."* In *Black Literature and Literary Theory,* edited by Henry Louis Gates, Jr., pp. 205–21. New York: Methuen, 1984.

————. "Thresholds of Difference: Structures of Address in Zora Neale Hurston." In *"Race," Writing and Difference,* edited by Henry Lewis Gates, Jr. Chicago: University of Chicago Press, 1986.

Jordan, June. "On Richard Wright and Zora Neale Hurston." *Black World* 23 (10) (August 1974): 4–8.

Kubitschek, Missy Dehn. " 'Tuh de Horizon and Back': The Female Quest in *Their Eyes." Black American Literature Forum* 17 (3) (Fall 1983): 109–15.

Lionnet, Françoise. "Autoethnography: The Anarchic Style of *Dust Tracks on a Road."* In Françoise Lionnet, *Autobiographical Voices: Race, Gender, Self-Portraiture,* pp. 97–130. Ithaca: Cornell University Press, 1989.

Lupton, Mary Jane. "Zora Neale Hurston and the Survival of the Female." *Southern Literary Journal* 15 (Fall 1982): 45–54.

Meese, Elizabeth. "Orality and Textuality in Zora Neale Hurston's *Their Eyes."* In Elizabeth Meese, *Crossing the Double Cross: The Practice of Feminist Criticism,* pp. 39–55. Chapel Hill: University of North Carolina Press, 1986.

Newson, Adele S. *Zora Neale Hurston: A Reference Guide.* Boston: G. K. Hall, 1987.

Rayson, Ann. *"Dust Tracks on a Road:* Zora Neale Hurston and the Form of Black Autobiography." *Negro American Literature Forum* 7 (Summer 1973): 42–44.

Sheffey, Ruthe T., ed. *A Rainbow Round Her Shoulder: The Zora Neale Hurston Symposium Papers.* Baltimore: Morgan State University Press, 1982.

Smith, Barbara. "Sexual Politics and the Fiction of Zora Neale Hurston." *Radical Teacher* 8 (May 1978): 26–30.

Stepto, Robert B. *From Behind the Veil.* Urbana: University of Illinois Press, 1979.

Walker, Alice. "In Search of Zora Neale Hurston." *Ms.,* March 1975, pp. 74–79, 85–89.

Wall, Cheryl A. "Zora Neale Hurston: Changing Her Own Words." In *American Novelists Revisited: Essays in Feminist Criticism,* edited by Fritz Fleischmann, pp. 370–93. Boston: G. K. Hall, 1982.

Washington, Mary Helen. "Zora Neale Hurston: A Woman Half in Shadow." Introduction to *I Love Myself When I Am Laughing,* edited by Alice Walker. Old Westbury, N.Y.: Feminist Press, 1979.

————. " 'I Love the Way Janie Crawford Left Her Husbands': Zora Neale Hurston's Emergent Female Hero." In Mary Helen Washington, *Invented*

Lives: Narratives of Black Women, 1860–1960. New York: Anchor Press, 1987.

Willis, Miriam. "Folklore and the Creative Artist: Lydia Cabrera and Zora Neale Hurston." *CLA Journal* 27 (September 1983): 81–90.

Wolff, Maria Tai. "Listening and Living: Reading and Experience in *Their Eyes.*" *BALF* 16 (1) (Spring 1982): 29–33.

CHRONOLOGY

January 7, 1891	Born in Eatonville, Florida, the fifth of eight children, to John Hurston, a carpenter and Baptist preacher, and Lucy Potts Hurston, a former schoolteacher.
September 1917–June 1918	Attends Morgan Academy in Baltimore, completing the high school requirements.
Summer 1918	Works as a waitress in a nightclub and a manicurist in a black-owned barbershop that serves only whites.
1918–19	Attends Howard Prep School, Washington, D.C.
1919–24	Attends Howard University; receives an associate degree in 1920.
1921	Publishes her first story, "John Redding Goes to Sea," in the *Stylus,* the campus literary society's magazine.
December 1924	Publishes "Drenched in Light," a short story, in *Opportunity.*
1925	Submits a story, "Spunk," and a play, *Color Struck,* to *Opportunity*'s literary contest. Both win second-place awards; publishes "Spunk" in the June number.
1925–27	Attends Barnard College, studying anthropology with Franz Boas.
1926	Begins field work for Boas in Harlem.

January 1926	Publishes "John Redding Goes to Sea" in *Opportunity.*
Summer 1926	Organizes *Fire!* with Langston Hughes and Wallace Thurman; they publish only one issue, in November 1926. The issue includes Hurston's "Sweat."
August 1926	Publishes "Muttsy" in *Opportunity.*
September 1926	Publishes "Possum or Pig" in the *Forum.*
September– November 1926	Publishes "The Eatonville Anthology" in the *Messenger.*
1927	Publishes *The First One,* a play, in Charles S. Johnson's *Ebony and Topaz.*
February 1927	Goes to Florida to collect folklore.
May 19, 1927	Marries Herbert Sheen.
September 1927	First visits Mrs. Rufus Osgood Mason, seeking patronage.
October 1927	Publishes an account of the black settlement at St. Augustine, Florida, in the *Journal of Negro History;* also in this issue: "Cudjo's Own Story of the Last African Slaver."
December 1927	Signs a contract with Mason, enabling her to return to the South to collect folklore.
1928	Satirized as "Sweetie Mae Carr" in Wallace Thurman's novel about the Harlem Renaissance *Infants of the Spring;* receives a bachelor of arts degree from Barnard.
January 1928	Relations with Sheen break off.
May 1928	Publishes "How It Feels to Be Colored Me" in the *World Tomorrow.*
1930–32	Organizes the field notes that become *Mules and Men.*
May–June 1930	Works on the play *Mule Bone* with Langston Hughes.
1931	Publishes "Hoodoo in America" in the *Journal of American Folklore.*
February 1931	Breaks with Langston Hughes over the authorship of *Mule Bone.*
July 7, 1931	Divorces Sheen.

September 1931	Writes for a theatrical revue called *Fast and Furious*.
January 1932	Writes and stages a theatrical revue called *The Great Day,* first performed on January 10 on Broadway at the John Golden Theatre; works with the creative literature department of Rollins College, Winter Park, Florida, to produce a concert program of Negro music.
1933	Writes "The Fiery Chariot."
January 1933	Stages *From Sun to Sun* (a version of *Great Day*) at Rollins College.
August 1933	Publishes "The Gilded Six-Bits" in *Story.*
1934	Publishes six essays in Nancy Cunard's anthology, *Negro.*
January 1934	Goes to Bethune-Cookman College to establish a school of dramatic arts "based on pure Negro expression."
May 1934	Publishes *Jonah's Gourd Vine,* originally titled *Big Nigger;* it is a Book-of-the-Month Club selection.
September 1934	Publishes "The Fire and the Cloud" in the *Challenge.*
November 1934	*Singing Steel* (a version of *Great Day*) performed in Chicago.
January 1935	Makes an abortive attempt to study for a Ph.D. in anthropology at Columbia University on a fellowship from the Rosenwald Foundation. In fact, she seldom attends classes.
August 1935	Joins the WPA Federal Theatre Project as a "dramatic coach."
October 1935	*Mules and Men* published.
March 1936	Awarded a Guggenheim Fellowship to study West Indian Obeah practices.
April–September 1936	In Jamaica.
September–March 1937	In Haiti; writes *Their Eyes Were Watching God* in seven weeks.
May 1937	Returns to Haiti on a renewed Guggenheim.
September 1937	Returns to the United States; *Their Eyes Were Watching God* published, September 18.

February–March 1938.	Writes *Tell My Horse;* it is published the same year.
April 1938	Joins the Federal Writers Project in Florida to work on *The Florida Negro.*
1939	Publishes "Now Take Noses" in *Cordially Yours.*
June 1939	Receives an honorary Doctor of Letters degree from Morgan State College.
June 27, 1939	Marries Albert Price III in Florida.
Summer 1939	Hired as a drama instructor by North Carolina College for Negroes at Durham; meets Paul Green, professor of drama, at the University of North Carolina.
November 1939	*Moses, Man of the Mountain* published.
February 1940	Files for divorce from Price, though the two are reconciled briefly.
Summer 1940	Makes a folklore-collecting trip to South Carolina.
Spring–July 1941	Writes *Dust Tracks on a Road.*
July 1941	Publishes "Cock Robin, Beale Street" in the *Southern Literary Messenger.*
October 1941–January 1942	Works as a story consultant at Paramount Pictures.
July 1942	Publishes "Story in Harlem Slang" in the *American Mercury.*
September 5, 1942	Publishes a profile of Lawrence Silas in the *Saturday Evening Post.*
November 1942	*Dust Tracks on a Road* published.
February 1943	Awarded the Anisfield-Wolf Book Award in Race Relations for *Dust Tracks;* on the cover of the *Saturday Review.*
March 1943	Receives Howard University's Distinguished Alumni Award.
May 1943	Publishes "The 'Pet Negro' Syndrome" in the *American Mercury.*
November 1943	Divorce from Price granted.
June 1944	Publishes "My Most Humiliating Jim Crow Experience" in the *Negro Digest.*
1945	Writes *Mrs. Doctor;* it is rejected by Lippincott.

March 1945	Publishes "The Rise of the Begging Joints" in the *American Mercury.*
December 1945	Publishes "Crazy for This Democracy" in the *Negro Digest.*
1947	Publishes a review of Robert Tallant's *Voodoo in New Orleans* in the *Journal of American Folklore.*
May 1947	Goes to British Honduras to research black communities in Central America; writes *Seraph on the Suwanee;* stays in Honduras until March 1948.
September 1948	Falsely accused of molesting a ten-year-old boy and arrested; case finally dismissed in March 1949.
October 1948	*Seraph on the Suwanee* published.
March 1950	Publishes "Conscience of the Court" in the *Saturday Evening Post,* while working as a maid in Rivo Island, Florida.
April 1950	Publishes "What White Publishers Won't Print" in the *Saturday Evening Post.*
November 1950	Publishes "I Saw Negro Votes Peddled" in the *American Legion* magazine.
Winter 1950–51	Moves to Belle Glade, Florida.
June 1951	Publishes "Why the Negro Won't Buy Communism" in the *American Legion* magazine.
December 8, 1951	Publishes "A Negro Voter Sizes Up Taft" in the *Saturday Evening Post.*
1952	Hired by the *Pittsburgh Courier* to cover the Ruby McCollum case.
May 1956	Receives an award for "education and human relations" at Bethune-Cookman College.
June 1956	Works as a librarian at Patrick Air Force Base in Florida; fired in 1957.
1957–59	Writes a column on "Hoodoo and Black Magic" for the *Fort Pierce Chronicle.*
1958	Works as a substitute teacher at Lincoln Park Academy, Fort Pierce.
Early 1959	Suffers a stroke.
October 1959	Forced to enter the St. Lucie County Welfare Home.

January 28, 1960	Dies in the St. Lucie County Welfare Home of "hypertensive heart disease"; buried in an unmarked grave in the Garden of Heavenly Rest, Fort Pierce.
August 1973	Alice Walker discovers and marks Hurston's grave.
March 1975	Walker publishes "In Search of Zora Neale Hurston," in *Ms.,* launching a Hurston revival.